HELEN OF TROY

HELEN OF TROY

ANDREW LANG

WILDSIDE PRESS

HELEN OF TROY

Published by Wildside Press
P.O. Box 301
Holicong, PA 18928-0301
www.wildsidepress.com

First Wildside Press edition: 2003

HELEN OF TROY

"Le joyeulx temps passe souloit estre occasion que je faisoie de plaisants diz et gracieuses chanconnetes et ballades. Mais je me suis mis a faire cette traittie d'affliction contre ma droite nature . . . et suis content de l'avoir prinse, car mes douleurs me semblent en estre allegees."
—Le Romant de Troilus.

To all old Friends; to all who dwell
   Where Avon dhu and Avon gel
   Down to the western waters flow
Through valleys dear from long ago;
To all who hear the whisper'd spell
Of Ken; and Tweed like music swell
Hard by the Land Debatable,
   Or gleaming Shannon seaward go,—
     To all old Friends!

To all that yet remember well
What secrets Isis had to tell,
   How lazy Cherwell loiter'd slow
   Sweet aisles of blossom'd May below—
Whate'er befall, whate'er befell,
     To all old Friends.

BOOK I
THE COMING OF PARIS.

Of the coming of Paris to the house of Menelaus, King of Lacedaemon, and of the tale Paris told concerning his past life.

I.

All day within the palace of the King
    In Lacedaemon, was there revelry,
Since Menelaus with the dawn did spring
    Forth from his carven couch, and, climbing high
    The tower of outlook, gazed along the dry
White road that runs to Pylos through the plain,
    And mark'd thin clouds of dust against the sky,
And gleaming bronze, and robes of purple stain.

II.

Then cried he to his serving men, and all
    Obey'd him, and their labour did not spare,
And women set out tables through the hall,
    Light polish'd tables, with the linen fair.
    And water from the well did others bear,
And the good house-wife busily brought forth
    Meats from her store, and stinted not the rare
Wine from Ismarian vineyards of the North.

III.

The men drave up a heifer from the field
    For sacrifice, and sheath'd her horns with gold;
And strong Boethous the axe did wield
    And smote her; on the fruitful earth she roll'd,
    And they her limbs divided; fold on fold
They laid the fat, and cast upon the fire
    The barley grain. Such rites were wrought of old
When all was order'd as the Gods desire.

IV.

And now the chariots came beneath the trees
    Hard by the palace portals, in the shade,
And Menelaus knew King Diocles
    Of Pherae, sprung of an unhappy maid
    Whom the great Elian River God betray'd
In the still watches of a summer night,
    When by his deep green water-course she stray'd
And lean'd to pluck his water-lilies white.

V.

Besides King Diocles there sat a man
    Of all men mortal sure the fairest far,
For o'er his purple robe Sidonian
    His yellow hair shone brighter than the star
    Of the long golden locks that bodeth war;
His face was like the sunshine, and his blue
    Glad eyes no sorrow had the spell to mar
Were clear as skies the storm hath thunder'd through.

VI.

Then Menelaus spake unto his folk,
    And eager at his word they ran amain,
And loosed the sweating horses from the yoke,
    And cast before them spelt, and barley grain.
    And lean'd the polish'd car, with golden rein,
Against the shining spaces of the wall;
    And called the sea-rovers who follow'd fain
Within the pillar'd fore-courts of the hall.

VII.

The stranger-prince was follow'd by a band
    Of men, all clad like rovers of the sea,
And brown'd were they as is the desert sand,
    Loud in their mirth, and of their bearing free;
    And gifts they bore, from the deep treasury
And forests of some far-off Eastern lord,
    Vases of gold, and bronze, and ivory,
That might the Pythian fane have over-stored.

VIII.

Now when the King had greeted Diocles
    And him that seem'd his guest, the twain were led
To the dim polish'd baths, where, for their ease,
    Cool water o'er their lustrous limbs was shed;
    With oil anointed was each goodly head
By Asteris and Phylo fair of face;
    Next, like two gods for loveliness, they sped
To Menelaus in the banquet-place.

IX.

There were they seated at the King's right hand,
    And maidens bare them bread, and meat, and wine,
Within that fair hall of the Argive land
    Whose doors and roof with gold and silver shine
    As doth the dwelling-place of Zeus divine.
And Helen came from forth her fragrant bower
    The fairest lady of immortal line,
Like morning, when the rosy dawn doth flower.

X.

Adraste set for her a shining chair,
    Well-wrought of cedar-wood and ivory;
And beautiful Alcippe led the fair,
    The well-beloved child, Hermione,—
    A little maiden of long summers three—
Her star-like head on Helen's breast she laid,
    And peep'd out at the strangers wistfully
As is the wont of children half afraid.

XI.

Now when desire of meat and drink was done,
    And ended was the joy of minstrelsy,
Queen Helen spake, beholding how the sun
    Within the heaven of bronze was riding high:
    "Truly, my friends, methinks the hour is nigh
When men may crave to know what need doth bring
    To Lacedaemon, o'er wet ways and dry,
This prince that bears the sceptre of a king?

XII.

"Yea, or perchance a God is he, for still
    The great Gods wander on our mortal ways,
And watch their altars upon mead or hill
    And taste our sacrifice, and hear our lays,
    And now, perchance, will heed if any prays,
And now will vex us with unkind control,
    But anywise must man live out his days,
For Fate hath given him an enduring soul.

XIII.

"Then tell us, prithee, all that may be told,
    And if thou art a mortal, joy be thine!
And if thou art a God, then rich with gold
    Thine altar in our palace court shall shine,
    With roses garlanded and wet with wine,
And we shall praise thee with unceasing breath;
    Ah, then be gentle as thou art divine,
And bring not on us baneful Love or Death!"

XIV.

Then spake the stranger,—as when to a maid
    A young man speaks, his voice was soft and low,—
"Alas, no God am I; be not afraid,
    For even now the nodding daisies grow
    Whose seed above my grassy cairn shall blow,
When I am nothing but a drift of white
    Dust in a cruse of gold; and nothing know
But darkness, and immeasurable Night.

XV.

"The dawn, or noon, or twilight, draweth near
    When one shall smite me on the bridge of war,
Or with the ruthless sword, or with the spear,
    Or with the bitter arrow flying far.
    But as a man's heart, so his good days are,
That Zeus, the Lord of Thunder, giveth him,
    Wherefore I follow Fortune, like a star,
Whate'er may wait me in the distance dim.

XVI.

"Now all men call me *Paris, Priam's son,*
    Who widely rules a peaceful folk and still.
Nay, though ye dwell afar off, there is none
    But hears of Ilios on the windy hill,
    And of the plain that the two rivers fill
With murmuring sweet streams the whole year long,
    And walls the Gods have wrought with wondrous skill
Where cometh never man to do us wrong.

XVII.

"Wherefore I sail'd not here for help in war,
　　Though well the Argives in such need can aid.
The force that comes on me is other far;
　　One that on all men comes: I seek the maid
　　Whom golden Aphrodite shall persuade
To lay her hand in mine, and follow me,
　　To my white halls within the cedar shade
Beyond the waters of the barren sea."

XVIII.

Then at the Goddess' name grew Helen pale,
　　Like golden stars that flicker in the dawn,
Or like a child that hears a dreadful tale,
　　Or like the roses on a rich man's lawn,
　　When now the suns of Summer are withdrawn,
And the loose leaves with a sad wind are stirr'd,
　　Till the wet grass is strewn with petals wan,—
So paled the golden Helen at his word.

XIX.

But swift the rose into her cheek return'd
　　And for a little moment, like a flame,
The perfect face of Argive Helen burn'd,
　　As doth a woman's, when some spoken name
　　Brings back to mind some ancient love or shame,
But none save Paris mark'd the thing, who said,
　　"My tale no more must weary this fair dame,
With telling why I wander all unwed."

XX.

But Helen, bending on him gracious brows,
　　Besought him for the story of his quest,
"For sultry is the summer, that allows
　　To mortal men no sweeter boon than rest;
　　And surely such a tale as thine is best
To make the dainty-footed hours go by,
　　Till sinks the sun in darkness and the West,
And soft stars lead the Night along the sky."

XXI.

Then at the word of Helen Paris spoke,
    "My tale is shorter than a summer day,—
My mother, ere I saw the light, awoke,
    At dawn, in Ilios, shrieking in dismay,
    Who dream'd that 'twixt her feet there fell and lay
A flaming brand, that utterly burn'd down
    To dust of crumbling ashes red and grey,
The coronal of towers and all Troy town.

XXII.

"Then the interpretation of this dream
    My father sought at many priestly hands,
Where the white temple doth in Pytho gleam,
    And at the fane of Ammon in the sands,
    And where the oak tree of Dodona stands
With boughs oracular against the sky,—
    And with one voice the Gods from all the lands,
Cried out, 'The child must die, the child must die.'

XXIII.

"Then was I born to sorrow; and in fear
    The dark priest took me from my sire, and bore
A wailing child through beech and pinewood drear,
    Up to the knees of Ida, and the hoar
    Rocks whence a fountain breaketh evermore,
And leaps with shining waters to the sea,
    Through black and rock-wall'd pools without a shore,—
And there they deem'd they took farewell of me.

XXIV.

"But 'round my neck they tied a golden ring
    That fell from Ganymedes when he soar'd
High over Ida on the eagle's wing,
    To dwell for ever with the Gods adored,
    To be the cup-bearer beside the board
Of Zeus, and kneel at the eternal throne,—
    A jewel 'twas from old King Tros's hoard,
That ruled in Ilios ages long agone.

XXV.

"And there they left me in that dell untrod,—
    Shepherd nor huntsman ever wanders there,
For dread of Pan, that is a jealous God,—
    Yea, and the ladies of the streams forbear
    The Naiad nymphs, to weave their dances fair,
Or twine their yellow tresses with the shy
    Fronds of forget-me-not and maiden-hair,—
There had the priests appointed me to die.

XXVI.

"But vainly doth a man contend with Fate!
    My father had less pity on his son
Than wild things of the woodland desolate.
    'Tis said that ere the Autumn day was done
    A great she-bear, that in these rocks did wonn,
Beheld a sleeping babe she did convey
    Down to a den beheld not of the sun,
The cavern where her own soft litter lay.

XXVII.

"And therein was I nurtured wondrously,
    So Rumour saith: I know not of these things,
For mortal men are ever wont to lie,
    Whene'er they speak of sceptre-bearing kings:
    I tell what I was told, for memory brings
No record of those days, that are as deep
    Lost as the lullaby a mother sings
In ears of children that are fallen on sleep.

XXVIII.

"Men say that now five autumn days had pass'd,
    When Agelaus, following a hurt deer,
Trod soft on crackling acorns, and the mast
    That lay beneath the oak and beech-wood sere,
    In dread lest angry Pan were sleeping near,
Then heard a cry from forth a cavern grey,
    And peeping 'round the fallen rocks in fear,
Beheld where in the wild beast's tracks I lay.

14

XXIX.

"So Agelaus bore me from the wild,
    Down to his hut; and with his children I
Was nurtured, being, as was deem'd, the child
    Of Hermes, or some mountain deity;
    For these with the wild nymphs are wont to lie
Within the holy caverns, where the bee
    Can scarcely find a darkling path to fly
Through veils of bracken and the ivy-tree.

XXX.

"So with the shepherds on the hills I stray'd,
    And drave the kine to feed where rivers run,
And play'd upon the reed-pipe in the shade,
    And scarcely knew my manhood was begun,
    The pleasant years still passing one by one,
Till I was chiefest of the mountain men,
    And clomb the peaks that take the snow and sun,
And braved the anger'd lion in his den.

XXXI.

"Now in my herd of kine was one more dear
    By far than all the rest, and fairer far;
A milkwhite bull, the captive of my spear,
    And all the wondering shepherds called him *Star:*
    And still he led his fellows to the war,
When the lean wolves against the herds came down,
    Then would he charge, and drive their hosts afar
Beyond the pastures to the forests brown.

XXXII.

"Now so it chanced that on an autumn morn,
    King Priam sought a goodly bull to slay
In memory of his child, no sooner born
    Than midst the lonely mountains cast away,
    To die ere scarce he had beheld the day;
And Priam's men came wandering afar
    To that green pool where by the flocks I lay,
And straight they coveted the goodly *Star,*

XXXIII.

"And drave him, no word spoken, to the town:
    One man mine arrow lit on, and he fell;
His comrades held me off, and down and down,
    Through golden windings of the autumn dell,
    They spurr'd along the beast that loved me well,
Till red were his white sides; I following,
    Wrath in my heart, their evil deeds to tell
In Ilios, at the footstool of the King.

XXXIV.

"But ere they came to the God-builded wall,
    They spied a meadow by the water-side,
And there the men of Troy were gathered all
    For joust and play; and Priam's sons defied
    All other men in all Maeonia wide
To strive with them in boxing and in speed.
    Victorious with the shepherds had I vied,
So boldly followed to that flowery mead.

XXXV.

"Maeonia, Phrygia, Troia there were met,
    And there the King, child of Laomedon,
Rich prizes for the vanquishers had set,
    Damsels, and robes, and cups that like the sun
    Shone, but the white bull was the chiefest one;
And him the victor in the games should slay
    To Zeus, the King of Gods, when all was done,
And so with sacrifice should crown the day.

XXXVI.

"Now it were over long, methinks, to tell
    The contest of the heady charioteers,
Of them the goal that turn'd, and them that fell.
    But I outran the young men of my years,
    And with the bow did I out-do my peers,
And wrestling; and in boxing, over-bold,
    I strove with Hector of the ashen spears,
Yea, till the deep-voiced Heralds bade us hold.

XXXVII.

"Then Priam hail'd me winner of the day;
  Mine were the maid, the cup, and chiefest prize,
Mine own fair milkwhite bull was mine to slay;
  But then the murmurs wax'd to angry cries,
  And hard men set on me in deadly wise,
My brethren, though they knew it not; I turn'd,
  And fled unto the place of sacrifice,
Where altars to the God of strangers burn'd.

XXXVIII.

"At mine own funeral feast, had I been slain,
  But, fearing Zeus, they halted for a space,
And lo, Apollo's priestess with a train
  Of holy maidens came into that place,
  And far did she outshine the rest in grace,
But in her eyes such dread was frozen then
  As glares eternal from the Gorgon's face
Wherewith Athene quells the ranks of men.

XXXIX.

"She was old Priam's daughter, long ago
  Apollo loved her, and did not deny
His gifts,—the things that are to be to know,
  The tongue of sooth-saying that cannot lie,
  And knowledge gave he of all birds that fly
'Neath heaven; and yet his prayer did she disdain.
  So he his gifts confounded utterly,
And sooth she saith, but evermore in vain.

XL.

"She, when her dark eyes fell on me, did stand
  At gaze a while, with wan lips murmuring,
And then came nigh to me, and took my hand,
  And led me to the footstool of the King,
  And call'd me 'brother,' and drew forth the ring
That men had found upon me in the wild,
  For still I bore it as a precious thing,
The token of a father to his child.

XLI.

"This sign Cassandra show'd to Priam: straight
    The King wax'd pale, and ask'd what this might be?
And she made answer, 'Sir, and King, thy fate
    That comes to all men born hath come on thee;
    This shepherd is thine own child verily:
How like to thine his shape, his brow, his hands!
    Nay there is none but hath the eyes to see
That here the child long lost to Troia stands.'

XLII.

"Then the King bare me to his lofty hall,
    And there we feasted in much love and mirth,
And Priam to the mountain sent for all
    That knew me, and the manner of my birth:
    And now among the great ones of the earth
In royal robe and state behold me set,
    And one fell thing I fear not; even dearth,
Whate'er the Gods remember or forget.

XLIII.

"My new rich life had grown a common thing,
    The pleasant years still passing one by one,
When deep in Ida was I wandering
    The glare of well-built Ilios to shun,
    In summer, ere the day was wholly done,
When I beheld a goodly prince,—the hair
    To bloom upon his lip had scarce begun,—
The season when the flower of youth is fair.

XLIV.

"Then knew I Hermes by his golden wand
    Wherewith he lulls the eyes of men to sleep;
But, nodding with his brows, he bade me stand,
    And spake, 'Tonight thou hast a tryst to keep,
    With Goddesses within the forest deep;
And Paris, lovely things shalt thou behold,
    More fair than they for which men war and weep,
Kingdoms, and fame, and victories, and gold.

XLV.

"'For, lo! tonight within the forest dim
    Do Aphrodite and Athene meet,
And Hera, who to thee shall bare each limb,
    Each grace from golden head to ivory feet,
    And thee, fair shepherd Paris, they entreat
As thou 'mongst men art beauteous, to declare
    Which Queen of Queens immortal is most sweet,
And doth deserve the meed of the most fair.

XLVI.

"'For late between them rose a bitter strife
    In Peleus' halls upon his wedding day,
When Peleus took him an immortal wife,
    And there was bidden all the God's array,
    Save Discord only; yet she brought dismay,
And cast an apple on the bridal board,
    With "Let the fairest bear the prize away"
Deep on its golden rind and gleaming scored.

XLVII.

"'Now in the sudden night, whenas the sun
    In Tethys' silver arms hath slept an hour,
Shalt thou be had into the forest dun,
    And brought unto a dark enchanted bower,
    And there of Goddesses behold the flower
With very beauty burning in the night,
    And these will offer Wisdom, Love, and Power;
Then, Paris, be thou wise, and choose aright!'

XLVIII.

"He spake, and pass'd, and Night without a breath,
    Without a star drew on; and now I heard
The voice that in the springtime wandereth,
    The crying of Dame Hera's shadowy bird;
    And soon the silence of the trees was stirred
By the wise fowl of Pallas; and anigh,
    More sweet than is a girl's first loving word,
The doves of Aphrodite made reply.

XLIX.

"These voices did I follow through the trees,
  Threading the coppice 'neath a starless sky,
When, lo! the very Queen of Goddesses,
  In golden beauty gleaming wondrously,
  Even she that hath the Heaven for canopy,
And in the arms of mighty Zeus doth sleep,—
  And then for dread methought that I must die,
But Hera called me with soft voice and deep:

L.

"'Paris, give me the prize, and thou shalt reign
  O'er many lordly peoples, far and wide,
From them that till the black and crumbling plain,
  Where the sweet waters of Aegyptus glide,
  To those that on the Northern marches ride,
And the Ceteians, and the blameless men
  That 'round the rising-place of Morn abide,
And all the dwellers in the Asian fen.

LI.

"'And I will love fair Ilios as I love
  Argos and rich Mycenae, that doth hoard
Deep wealth; and I will make thee king above
  A hundred peoples; men shall call thee lord
  In tongues thou know'st not; thou shalt be adored
With sacrifice, as are the Gods divine,
  If only thou wilt speak a little word,
And say the prize of loveliness is mine.'

LII.

"Then, as I doubted, like a sudden flame
  Of silver came Athene, and methought
Beholding her, how stately, as she came,
  That dim wood to a fragrant fane was wrought;
  So pure the warlike maiden seem'd, that nought
But her own voice commanding made me raise
  Mine eyes to see her beauty, who besought
In briefest words the guerdon of all praise.

LIII.

"She spake: 'Nor wealth nor crowns are in my gift;
　　But wisdom, but the eyes that glance afar,
But courage, and the spirit that is swift
　　　To cleave her path through all the waves of war;
　　　Endurance that the Fates can never mar;
These, and my loving friendship,—these are thine,
　　　And these shall guide thee, steadfast as a star,
If thou hast eyes to know the prize is mine.'

LIV.

"Last, in a lovely mist of rosy fire,
　　Came Aphrodite through the forest glade,
The queen of all delight and all desire,
　　　More fair than when her naked foot she laid
　　　On the blind mere's wild wave that sank dismay'd,
What time the sea grew smoother than a lake;
　　　I was too happy to be sore afraid.
And like a song her voice was when she spake:

LV.

"'Oh Paris, what is power? Tantalus
　　And Sisyphus were kings long time ago,
But now they lie in the Lake Dolorous,
　　　The hills of hell are noisy with their woe;
　　　Ay, swift the tides of Empire ebb and flow,
And that is quickly lost was hardly won,
　　　As Ilios herself o'erwell did know
When high walls help'd not King Laomedon.

LVI.

"'And what are strength and courage? for the child
　　Of mighty Zeus, the strong man Herakles,
Knew many days and evil, ere men piled
　　　The pyre in Oeta, where he got his ease
　　　In death, where all the ills of brave men cease.
Nay, Love I proffer thee; beyond the brine
　　　Of all the currents of the Western seas,
The fairest woman in the world is thine!'

LVII.

"She spake, and touched the prize, and all grew dim
    I heard no voice of anger'd Deity,
But 'round me did the night air swoon and swim,
    And, when I waken'd, lo! the sun was high,
    And in that place accursed did I lie,
Where Agelaus found the naked child;
    Then with swift foot I did arise and fly
Forth from the deeps of that enchanted wild.

LVIII.

"And down I sped to Ilios, down the dell
    Where, years agone, the white bull guided me,
And through green boughs beheld where foam'd and fell
    The merry waters of the Western sea;
    Of Love the sweet birds sang from sky and tree,
And swift I reach'd the haven and the shore,
    And call'd my mariners, and follow'd free
Where Love might lead across the waters hoar.

LIX.

"Three days with fair winds ran we, then we drave
    Before the North that made the long waves swell
Round Malea; but hardly from the wave
    We 'scaped at Pylos, Nestor's citadel;
    And there the son of Neleus loved us well,
And brought us to the high prince, Diocles,
    Who led us hither, and it thus befell
That here, below thy roof, we sit at ease."

LX.

Then all men gave the stranger thanks and praise,
    And Menelaus for red wine bade call;
And the sun fell, and dark were all the ways;
    Then maidens set forth braziers in the hall,
    And heap'd them high with lighted brands withal;
But Helen pass'd, as doth the fading day
    Pass from the world, and softly left them all
Loud o'er their wine amid the twilight grey.

LXI.

So night drew on with rain, nor yet they ceased
    Within the hall to drink the gleaming wine,
And late they pour'd the last cup of the feast,
    To Argus-bane, the Messenger divine;
      And last, 'neath torches tall that smoke and shine,
The maidens strew'd the beds with purple o'er,
    That Diocles and Paris might recline
All night, beneath the echoing corridor.

BOOK II
THE SPELL OF APHRODITE.

The coming of Aphrodite, and how she told Helen that she must depart in company with Paris, but promised withal that Helen, having fallen into a deep sleep, should awake forgetful of her old life, and ignorant of her shame, and blameless of those evil deeds that the Goddess thrust upon her.

I.

Now in the upper chamber o'er the gate
    Lay Menelaus on his carven bed,
And swift and sudden as the stroke of Fate
    A deep sleep fell upon his weary head.
    But the soft-winged God with wand of lead
Came not near Helen; wistful did she lie,
    Till dark should change to grey, and grey to red,
And golden throned Morn sweep o'er the sky.

II.

Slow pass'd the heavy night: like one who fears
    The step of murder, she lies quivering,
If any cry of the night bird she hears;
    And strains her eyes to mark some dreadful thing,
    If but the curtains of the window swing,
Stirr'd by the breath of night, and still she wept
    As she were not the daughter of a king,
And no strong king, her lord, beside her slept.

III.

Now in that hour, the folk who watch the night,
    Shepherds and fishermen, and they that ply
Strange arts and seek their spells in the star-light,
    Beheld a marvel in the sea and sky,
    For all the waves of all the seas that sigh
Between the straits of Helle and the Nile,
    Flush'd with a flame of silver suddenly,
From soft Cythera to the Cyprian isle.

IV.

And Hesperus, the kindest star of heaven,
    That bringeth all things good, wax'd pale, and straight
There fell a flash of white malignant levin
    Among the gleaming waters desolate;
    The lights of sea and sky did mix and mate
And change to rosy flame, and thence did fly
    The lovely Queen of Love that turns to hate,
Like summer lightnings 'twixt the sea and sky.

V.

And now the bower of Helen fill'd with light,
    And now she knew the thing that she did fear
Was close upon her (for the black of night
    Doth burn like fire, whene'er the Gods are near);
    Then shone like flame each helm and shield and spear
That hung within the chamber of the King,
    But he,—though all the bower as day was clear,—
Slept as they sleep that know no wakening.

VI.

But Helen leap'd from her fair carven bed
    As some tormented thing that fear makes bold,
And on the ground she beat her golden head
    And pray'd with bitter moanings manifold.
    Yet knew that she could never move the cold
Heart of the lovely Goddess, standing there,
    Her feet upon a little cloud, a fold
Of silver cloud about her bosom bare.

VII.

So stood Queen Aphrodite, as she stands
    Unmoved in her bright mansion, when in vain
Some naked maiden stretches helpless hands
    And shifts the magic wheel, and burns the grain,
    And cannot win her lover back again,
Nor her old heart of quiet any more,
    Where moonlight floods the dim Sicilian main,
And the cool wavelets break along the shore.

VIII.

Then Helen ceased from unavailing prayer,
    And rose and faced the Goddess steadily,
Till even the laughter-loving lady fair
    Half shrank before the anger of her eye,
    And Helen cried with an exceeding cry,
"Why does Zeus live, if we indeed must be
    No more than sullen spoils of destiny,
And slaves of an adulteress like thee?

IX.

"What wilt thou with me, mistress of all woe?
    Say, wilt thou bear me to another land
Where thou hast other lovers? Rise and go
    Where dark the pine trees upon Ida stand,
    For there did one unloose thy girdle band;
Or seek the forest where Adonis bled,
    Or wander, wander on the yellow sand,
Where thy first lover strew'd thy bridal bed.

X.

"Ah, thy first lover! who is first or last
    Of men and gods, unnumber'd and unnamed?
Lover by lover in the race is pass'd,
    Lover by lover, outcast and ashamed.
    Oh, thou of many names, and evil famed!
What wilt thou with me? What must I endure
    Whose soul, for all thy craft, is never tamed?
Whose heart, for all thy wiles, is ever pure?

XI.

"Behold, my heart is purer than the plume
    Upon the stainless pinions of the swan,
And thou wilt smirch and stain it with the fume
    Of all thy hateful lusts Idalian.
    My name shall be a hissing that a man
Shall smile to speak, and women curse and hate,
    And on my little child shall come a ban,
And all my lofty home be desolate.

XII.

"Is it thy will that like a golden cup
    From lip to lip of heroes I must go,
And be but as a banner lifted up,
    To beckon where the winds of war may blow?
    Have I not seen fair Athens in her woe,
And all her homes aflame from sea to sea,
    When my fierce brothers wrought her overthrow
Because Athenian Theseus carried me—

XIII.

"Me, in my bloomless youth, a maiden child,
  From Artemis' pure altars and her fane,
And bare me, with Pirithous the wild
  To rich Aphidna? Many a man was slain,
  And wet with blood the fair Athenian plain,
And fired was many a goodly temple then,
  But fire nor blood can purify the stain
Nor make my name reproachless among men."

XIV.

Then Helen ceased, her passion like a flame
  That slays the thing it lives by, blazed and fell,
As faint as waves at dawn, though fierce they came,
  By night to storm some rocky citadel;
  For Aphrodite answer'd,—like a spell
Her voice makes strength of mortals pass away,—
  "Dost thou not know that I have loved thee well,
And never loved thee better than today?

XV.

"Behold, thine eyes are wet, thy cheeks are wan,
  Yet art thou born of an immortal sire,
The child of Nemesis and of the Swan;
  Thy veins should run with ichor and with fire.
  Yet this is thy delight and thy desire,
To love a mortal lord, a mortal child,
  To live, unpraised of lute, unhymn'd of lyre,
As any woman pure and undefiled.

XVI.

"Thou art the toy of Gods, an instrument
  Wherewith all mortals shall be plagued or blest,
Even at my pleasure; yea, thou shalt be bent
  This way and that, howe'er it like me best:
  And following thee, as tides the moon, the West
Shall flood the Eastern coasts with waves of war,
  And thy vex'd soul shall scarcely be at rest,
Even in the havens where the deathless are.

XVII.

"The instruments of men are blind and dumb,
  And this one gift I give thee, to be blind
And heedless of the thing that is to come,
  And ignorant of that which is behind;
  Bearing an innocent forgetful mind
In each new fortune till I visit thee
  And stir thy heart, as lightning and the wind
Bear fire and tumult through a sleeping sea.

XVIII.

"Thou shalt forget Hermione; forget
  Thy lord, thy lofty palace, and thy kin;
Thy hand within a stranger's shalt thou set,
  And follow him, nor deem it any sin;
  And many a strange land wand'ring shalt thou win,
And thou shalt come to an unhappy town,
  And twenty long years shalt thou dwell therein,
Before the Argives mar its towery crown.

XIX.

"And of thine end I speak not, but thy name,—
  Thy name which thou lamentest,—that shall be
A song in all men's speech, a tongue of flame
  Between the burning lips of Poesy;
  And the nine daughters of Mnemosyne,
With Prince Apollo, leader of the nine,
  Shall make thee deathless in their minstrelsy!
Yea, for thou shalt outlive the race divine,

XX.

"The race of Gods, for like the sons of men
  We Gods have but our season, and go by;
And Cronos pass'd, and Uranus, and then
  Shall Zeus and all his children utterly
  Pass, and new Gods be born, and reign, and die,—
But thee shall lovers worship evermore
  What Gods soe'er usurp the changeful sky,
Or flit to the irremeable shore.

XXI.

"Now sleep and dream not, sleep the long day through,
  And the brief watches of the summer night,
And then go forth amid the flowers and dew,
  Where the red rose of Dawn outburns the white.
  Then shalt thou learn my mercy and my might
Between the drowsy lily and the rose;
  There shalt thou spell the meaning of delight,
And know such gladness as a Goddess knows!"

XXII.

Then Sleep came floating from the Lemnian isle,
  And over Helen crush'd his poppy crown,
Her soft lids waver'd for a little while,
  Then on her carven bed she laid her down,
  And Sleep, the comforter of king and clown,
Kind Sleep the sweetest, near akin to Death,
  Held her as close as Death doth men that drown,
So close that none might hear her inward breath—

XXIII.

So close no man might tell she was not dead!
  And then the Goddess took her zone,—where lies
All her enchantment, love and lustihead,
  And the glad converse that beguiles the wise,
  And grace the very Gods may not despise,
And sweet Desire that doth the whole world move,—
  And therewith touch'd she Helen's sleeping eyes
And made her lovely as the Queen of Love.

XXIV.

Then laughter-loving Aphrodite went
  To far Idalia, over land and sea,
And scarce the fragrant cedar-branches bent
  Beneath her footsteps, faring daintily;
  And in Idalia the Graces three
Anointed her with oil ambrosial,—
  So to her house in Sidon wended she
To mock the prayers of lovers when they call.

XXV.

And all day long the incense and the smoke
    Lifted, and fell, and soft and slowly roll'd,
And many a hymn and musical awoke
    Between the pillars of her house of gold,
    And rose-crown'd girls, and fair boys linen-stoled,
Did sacrifice her fragrant courts within,
    And in dark chapels wrought rites manifold
The loving favour of the Queen to win.

XXVI.

But Menelaus, waking suddenly,
    Beheld the dawn was white, the day was near,
And rose, and kiss'd fair Helen; no good-bye
    He spake, and never mark'd a fallen tear,—
    Men know not when they part for many a year,—
He grasp'd a bronze-shod lance in either hand,
    And merrily went forth to drive the deer,
With Paris, through the dewy morning land.

XXVII.

So up the steep sides of Taygetus
    They fared, and to the windy hollows came,
While from the streams of deep Oceanus
    The sun arose, and on the fields did flame;
    And through wet glades the huntsmen drave the game,
And with them Paris sway'd an ashen spear,
    Heavy, and long, and shod with bronze to tame
The mountain-dwelling goats and forest deer.

XXVIII.

Now in a copse a mighty boar there lay,
    For through the boughs the wet winds never blew,
Nor lit the bright sun on it with his ray,
    Nor rain might pierce the woven branches through,
    But leaves had fallen deep the lair to strew:
Then questing of the hounds and men's foot-fall
    Aroused the boar, and forth he sprang to view,
With eyes that burn'd, at bay, before them all.

XXIX.

Then Paris was the first to rush on him,
    With spear aloft in his strong hand to smite,
And through the monster pierced the point; and dim
    The flame fell in his eyes, and all his might
    With his last cry went forth; forgetting fight,
Forgetting strength, he fell, and gladly then
    They gather'd 'round, and dealt with him aright;
Then left his body with the serving men.

XXX.

Now birds were long awake, that with their cry
    Were wont to waken Helen; and the dew
Where fell the sun upon the lawn was dry,
    And all the summer land was glad anew;
    And maidens' footsteps rang the palace through,
And with their footsteps chimed their happy song,
    And one to other cried, "A marvel new
That soft-wing'd Sleep hath held the Queen so long!"

XXXI.

Then Phylo brought the child Hermione,
    And close unto her mother's side she crept,
And o'er her god-like beauty tumbled she,
    Chiding her sweetly that so late she slept,
    And babbling still a merry coil she kept;
But like a woman stiff beneath her shroud
    Lay Helen; till the young child fear'd and wept,
And ran, and to her nurses cried aloud.

XXXII.

Then came the women quickly, and in dread
    Gather'd 'round Helen, but might naught avail
To wake her; moveless as a maiden dead
    That Artemis hath slain, yet nowise pale,
    She lay; but Aethra did begin the wail,
And all the women with sad voice replied,
    Who deem'd her pass'd unto the poplar vale
Wherein doth dread Persephone abide.

XXXIII.

Ah! slowly pass'd the miserable day
    In the rich house that late was full of pride;
Then the sun fell, and all the paths were grey,
    And Menelaus from the mountain-side
    Came, and through palace doors all open wide
Rang the wild dirge that told him of the thing
    That Helen, that the Queen had strangely died.
Then on his threshold fell he grovelling,

XXXIV.

And cast the dust upon his yellow hair,
    And, but that Paris leap'd and held his hand,
His hunter's knife would he have clutch'd, and there
    Had slain himself, to follow to that land
    Where flit the ghosts of men, a shadowy band
That have no more delight, no more desire,
    When once the flesh hath burn'd down like a brand,
Drench'd by the dark wine on the funeral pyre:

XXXV.

So on the ashen threshold lay the king,
    And all within the house was chill and drear;
The women watchers gather'd in a ring
    About the bed of Helen and her bier;
    And much had they to tell, and much to hear,
Of happy queens and fair, untimely dead,—
    Such joy they took amid their evil cheer,—
While the low thunder muttered overhead.

BOOK III

THE FLIGHT OF HELEN.

The flight of Helen and Paris from Lacedaemon, and of what things befell them in their voyaging, and how they came to Troy.

I.

The grey Dawn's daughter, rosy Morn awoke
    In old Tithonus' arms, and suddenly
Let harness her swift steeds beneath the yoke,
    And drave her shining chariot through the sky.
    Then men might see the flocks of Thunder fly,
All gold and rose, the azure pastures through,
    What time the lark was carolling on high
Above the gardens drench'd with rainy dew.

II.

But Aphrodite sent a slumber deep
    On all in the King's palace, young and old,
And one by one the women fell asleep,—
    Their lamentable tales left half untold,—
    Before the dawn, when folk wax weak and cold,
But Helen waken'd with the shining morn,
    Forgetting quite her sorrows manifold,
And light of heart as was the day new-born.

III.

She had no memory of unhappy things,
    She knew not of the evil days to come,
Forgotten were her ancient wanderings,
    And as Lethaean waters wholly numb
    The sense of spirits in Elysium,
That no remembrance may their bliss alloy,
    Even so the rumour of her days was dumb,
And all her heart was ready for new joy.

IV.

The young day knows not of an elder dawn,
    Joys of old noons, old sorrows of the night,
And so from Helen was the past withdrawn,
    Her lord, her child, her home forgotten quite,
    Lost in the marvel of a new delight:
She was as one who knows he shall not die,
    When earthly colours melt into the bright
Pure splendour of his immortality.

V.

Then Helen rose, and all her body fair
    She bath'd in the spring water, pure and cold,
And with her hand bound up her shining hair
    And clothed her in the raiment that of old
    Athene wrought with marvels manifold,
A bridal gift from an immortal hand,
    And all the front was clasp'd with clasps of gold,
And for the girdle was a golden band.

VI.

Next from her upper chamber silently
    Went Helen, moving like a morning dream.
She did not know the golden roof, the high
    Walls, and the shields that on the pillars gleam,
    Only she heard the murmur of the stream
That waters all the garden's wide expanse,
    This song, and cry of singing birds, did seem
To guide her feet as music guides the dance.

VII.

The music drew her on to the glad air
    From forth the chamber of enchanted death,
And lo! the world was waking everywhere;
    The wind went by, a cool delicious breath,
    Like that which in the gardens wandereth,
The golden gardens of the Hesperides,
    And in its song unheard of things it saith,
The myriad marvels of the fairy seas.

VIII.

So through the courtyard to the garden close
    Went Helen, where she heard the murmuring
Of water 'twixt the lily and the rose;
    For thereby doth a double fountain spring.
    To one stream do the women pitchers bring
By Menelaus' gates, at close of day;
    The other through the close doth shine and sing,
Then to the swift Eurotas fleets away.

IX.

And Helen sat her down upon the grass,
    And pluck'd the little daisies white and red,
And toss'd them where the running waters pass,
    To watch them racing from the fountain-head,
    And whirl'd about where little streams dispread;
And still with merry birds the garden rang,
    And, *marry, marry*, in their song they said,
Or so do maids interpret that they sang.

X.

Then stoop'd she down, and watch'd the crystal stream,
    And fishes poising where the waters ran,
And lo! upon the glass a golden gleam,
    And purple as of robes Sidonian,
    Then, sudden turning, she beheld a man,
That knelt beside her; as her own face fair
    Was his, and o'er his shoulders for a span
Fell the bright tresses of his yellow hair.

XI.

Then either look'd on other with amaze
    As each had seen a God; for no long while
They marvell'd, but as in the first of days,
    The first of men and maids did meet and smile,
    And Aphrodite did their hearts beguile,
So hands met hands, lips lips, with no word said
    Were they enchanted 'neath that leafy aisle,
And silently were woo'd, betroth'd, and wed.

XII.

Ah, slowly did their silence wake to words
    That scarce had more of meaning than the song
Pour'd forth of the innumerable birds
    That fill the palace gardens all day long;
    So innocent, so ignorant of wrong,
Was she, so happy each in other's eyes,
    Thus wrought the mighty Goddess that is strong,
Even to make naught the wisdom of the wise.

XIII.

Now in the midst of that enchanted place
  Right gladly had they linger'd all day through,
And fed their love upon each other's face,
  But Aphrodite had a counsel new,
  And silently to Paris' side she drew,
In guise of Aethra, whispering that the day
  Pass'd on, while his ship waited, and his crew
Impatient, in the narrow Gythian bay.

XIV.

For thither had she brought them by her skill;
  But Helen saw her not,—nay, who can see
A Goddess come or go against her will?
  Then Paris whisper'd, "Come, ah, Love, with me!
  Come to a shore beyond the barren sea;
There doth the bridal crown await thy head,
  And there shall all the land be glad of thee!"
Then, like a child, she follow'd where he led.

XV.

For, like a child's her gentle heart was glad.
  So through the courtyard pass'd they to the gate;
And even there, as Aphrodite bade,
  The steeds of Paris and the chariots wait;
  Then to the well-wrought car he led her straight,
And grasped the shining whip and golden rein,
  And swift they drave until the day was late
By clear Eurotas through the fruitful plain.

XVI.

But now within the halls the magic sleep
  Was broken, and men sought them everywhere;
Yet Aphrodite cast a cloud so deep
  About their chariot none might see them there.
  And strangely did they hear the trumpets blare,
And noise of racing wheels; yet saw they nought:
  Then died the sounds upon the distant air,
And safe they won the haven that they sought.

XVII.

Beneath a grassy cliff, beneath the down,
　　Where swift Eurotas mingles with the sea,
There climb'd the grey walls of a little town,
　　The sleepy waters wash'd it languidly,
　　For tempests in that haven might not be.
The isle across the inlet guarded all,
　　And the shrill winds that roam the ocean free
Broke and were broken on the rocky wall.

XVIII.

Then Paris did a point of hunting blow,
　　Nor yet the sound had died upon the hill
When 'round the isle they spied a scarlet prow,
　　And oars that flash'd into that haven still,
　　The oarsmen bending forward with a will,
And swift their black ship to the haven-side
　　They brought, and steer'd her in with goodly skill,
And bare on board the strange Achaean bride.

XIX.

Now while the swift ship through the waters clave,
　　All happy things that in the waters dwell,
Arose and gamboll'd on the glassy wave,
　　And Nereus led them with his sounding shell:
　　Yea, the sea-nymphs, their dances weaving well,
In the green water gave them greeting free.
　　Ah, long light linger'd, late the darkness fell,
That night, upon the isle of Cranae!

XX.

And Hymen shook his fragrant torch on high,
　　Till all its waves of smoke and tongues of flame,
Like clouds of rosy gold fulfill'd the sky;
　　And all the Nereids from the waters came,
　　Each maiden with a musical sweet name;
Doris, and Doto, and Amphithoe;
　　And their shrill bridal song of love and shame
Made music in the silence of the sea.

XXI.

For this was like that night of summer weather,
    When mortal men and maidens without fear,
And forest-nymphs, and forest-gods together,
    Do worship Pan in the long twilight clear.
    And Artemis this one night spares the deer,
And every cave and dell, and every grove
    Is glad with singing soft and happy cheer,
With laughter, and with dalliance, and with love.

                    *   *   *

XXII.

Now when the golden-throned Dawn arose
    To waken gods and mortals out of sleep,
Queen Aphrodite sent the wind that blows
    From fairy gardens of the Western deep.
    The sails are spread, the oars of Paris leap
Past many a headland, many a haunted fane:
    And, merrily all from isle to isle they sweep
O'er the wet ways across the barren plain.

XXIII.

By many an island fort, and many a haven
    They sped, and many a crowded arsenal:
They saw the loves of Gods and men engraven
    On friezes of Astarte's temple wall.
    They heard that ancient shepherd Proteus call
His flock from forth the green and tumbling lea,
    And saw white Thetis with her maidens all
Sweep up to high Olympus from the sea.

XXIV.

They saw the vain and weary toil of men,
    The ships that win the rich man all he craves;
They pass'd the red-prow'd barks Egyptian,
    And heard afar the moaning of the slaves
    Pent in the dark hot hold beneath the waves;
And scatheless the Sardanian fleets among
    They sail'd; by men that sow the sea with graves,
Bearing black fate to folk of alien tongue.

XXV.

Then all day long a rolling cloud of smoke
    Would hang on the sea-limits, faint and far,
But through the night the beacon-flame upbroke
    From some rich island-town begirt with war;
    And all these things could neither make nor mar
The joy of lovers wandering, but they
    Sped happily, and heedless of the star
That hung o'er their glad haven, far away.

XXVI.

The fisher-sentinel upon the height
    Watch'd them with vacant eyes, and little knew
They bore the fate of Troy; to him the bright
    Plashed waters, with the silver shining through
    When tunny shoals came cruising in the blue,
Was more than Love that doth the world unmake;
    And listless gazed he as the gulls that flew
And shriek'd and chatter'd in the vessel's wake.

XXVII.

So the wind drave them, and the waters bare
    Across the great green plain unharvested,
Till through an after-glow they knew the fair
    Faint rose of snow on distant Ida's head.
    And swifter then the joyous oarsmen sped;
But night was ended, and the waves were fire
    Beneath the fleet feet of a dawning red
Or ere they won the land of their desire.

XXVIII.

Now when the folk about the haven knew
    The scarlet prow of Paris, swift they ran
And the good ship within the haven drew,
    And merrily their welcoming began.
    But none the face of Helen dared to scan;
Their bold eyes fell before they had their fill,
    For all men deem'd her that Idalian
Who loved Anchises on the lonely hill.

XXIX.

But when her sweet smile and her gentleness
    And her kind speech had won them from dismay,
They changed their minds, and 'gan the Gods to bless
    Who brought to Ilios that happy day.
    And all the folk fair Helen must convey,
Crown'd like a bride, and clad with flame-hued pall,
    Through the rich plain, along the water-way
Right to the great gates of the Ilian wall.

XXX.

And through the vines they pass'd, where old and young
    Had no more heed of the glad vintaging,
But all unpluck'd the purple clusters hung,
    Nor more of Linus did the minstrel sing,
    For he and all the folk were following,
Wine-stain'd and garlanded, in merry bands,
    Like men when Dionysus came as king,
And led his revel from the sun-burnt lands,

XXXI.

So from afar the music and the shout
    Roll'd up to Ilios and the Scaean gate,
And at the sound the city folk came out
    And bore sweet Helen—such a fairy weight
    As none might deem the burden of Troy's fate—
Across the threshold of the town, and all
    Flock'd with her, where King Priam sat in state,
Girt by his elders, on the Ilian wall.

XXXII.

No man but knew him by his crown of gold,
    And golden-studded sceptre, and his throne;
Ay, strong he seem'd as those great kings of old,
    Whose image is eternal on the stone
    Won from the dust that once was Babylon;
But kind of mood was he withal, and mild,
    And when his eyes on Argive Helen shone,
He loved her as a father doth a child.

XXXIII.

Round him were set his peers, as Panthous,
    Antenor, and Agenor, hardly grey,
Scarce touch'd as yet with age, nor garrulous
    As are cicalas on a sunny day:
    Such might they be when years had slipp'd away,
And made them over-weak for war or joy,
    Content to watch the Leaguer as it lay
Beside the ships, beneath the walls of Troy.

XXXIV.

Then Paris had an easy tale to tell,
    Which then might win upon men's wond'ring ears,
Who deem'd that Gods with mortals deign to dwell,
    And that the water of the West enspheres
    The happy Isles that know not Death nor tears;
Yea, and though monsters do these islands guard,
    Yet men within their coasts had dwelt for years
Uncounted, with a strange love for reward.

XXXV.

And there had Paris ventured: so said he,—
    Had known the Sirens' song, and Circe's wile;
And in a cove of that Hesperian sea
    Had found a maiden on a lonely isle;
    A sacrifice, if so men might beguile
The wrath of some beast-god they worshipp'd there,
    But Paris, 'twixt the sea and strait defile,
Had slain the beast, and won the woman fair.

XXXVI.

Then while the happy people cried "Well done,"
    And Priam's heart was melted by the tale—
For Paris was his best-beloved son—
    Came a wild woman, with wet eyes, and pale
    Sad face, men look'd on when she cast her veil,
Not gladly; and none mark'd the thing she said,
    Yet must they hear her long and boding wail
That follow'd still, however fleet they fled.

XXXVII.

She was the priestess of Apollo's fane,
    Cassandra, and the God of prophecy
Spurr'd her to speak and rent her! but in vain
    She toss'd her wasted arms against the sky,
    And brake her golden circlet angrily,
And shriek'd that they had brought within the gate
    Helen, a serpent at their hearts to lie!
Helen, a hell of people, king, and state!

XXXVIII.

But ere the God had left her; ere she fell
    And foam'd among her maidens on the ground,
The air was ringing with a merry swell
    Of flute, and pipe, and every sweetest sound,
    In Aphrodite's fane, and all around
Were roses toss'd beneath the glimmering green
    Of that high roof, and Helen there was crown'd
The Goddess of the Trojans, and their Queen.

BOOK IV
THE DEATH OF CORYTHUS.

*How Helen was made an outcast by the Trojan women,
and how Œnone, the old love of Paris, sent her son
Corythus to him as her messenger, and how Paris slew
him unwittingly; and of the curses of Œnone, and
the coming of the Argive host against Troy.*

I.

For long in Troia was there peace and mirth,
    The pleasant hours still passing one by one;
And Helen joy'd at each fresh morning's birth,
    And almost wept at setting of the sun,
    For sorrow that the happy day was done;
Nor dream'd of years when she should hate the light,
    And mourn afresh for every day begun,
Nor fare abroad save shamefully by night.

II.

And Paris was not one to backward cast
    A fearful glance; nor pluck sour fruits of sin,
Half ripe; but seized all pleasures while they last,
    Nor boded evil ere ill days begin.
    Nay, nor lamented much when caught therein,
In each adventure always finding joy,
    And hopeful still through waves of war to win
By strength of Hector, and the star of Troy.

III.

Now as the storms drive white sea-birds afar
    Within green upland glens to seek for rest,
So rumours pale of an approaching war
    Were blown across the islands from the west:
    For Agamemnon summon'd all the best
From towns and tribes he ruled, and gave command
    That free men all should gather at his hest
Through coasts and islets of the Argive land.

IV.

Sidonian merchant-men had seen the fleet
    Black war-galleys that sped from town to town;
Had heard the hammers of the bronze-smiths beat
    The long day through, and when the sun went down;
    And thin, said they, would show the leafy crown
On many a sacred mountain-peak in spring,
    For men had fell'd the pine-trees tall and brown
To fashion them curved ships for seafaring.

V.

And still the rumour grew; for heralds came,
   Old men from Argos, bearing holy boughs,
Demanding great atonement for the shame
   And sore despite done Menelaus' house;
   But homeward soon they turn'd their scarlet prows,
And all their weary voyaging was vain;
   For Troy had bound herself with awful vows
To cleave to Helen till the walls were ta'en.

VI.

And now, like swallows ere the winter weather,
   The women in shrill groups were gathering,
With eager tongues still communing together,
   And many a taunt at Helen would they fling,
   Ay, through her innocence she felt the sting,
And shamed was now her gentle face and sweet,
   For e'en the children evil songs would sing
To mock her as she hasted down the street.

VII.

Also the men who worshipp'd her of old
   As she had been a goddess from above,
Gazed at her now with lustful eyes and bold,
   As she were naught but Paris' light-o'-love;
   And though in truth they still were proud enough,
Of that fair gem in their old city set,
   Yet well she knew that wanton word and scoff
Went 'round the camp-fire when the warriors met.

VIII.

There came a certain holiday when Troy
   Was wont to send her noble matrons all,
Young wives and old, with clamour and with joy,
   To clothe Athene in her temple hall,
   And robe her in a stately broider'd pall.
But now they drove fair Helen from their train,
   "Better," they scream'd, "to cast her from the wall,
Than mock the Gods with offerings in vain."

IX.

One joy she had, that Paris yet was true,
    Ay, fickle Paris, true unto the end;
And in the court of Ilios were two
    Kind hearts, still eager Helen to defend,
    And help and comfort in all need to lend:—
The gentle Hector with soft speech and mild,
    And the old king that ever was her friend,
And loved her as a father doth his child.

X.

These, though they knew not all, these blamed her not,
    But cast the heavy burden on the God,
Whose wrath, they deem'd, had verily waxed hot
    Against the painful race on earth that trod,
    And in God's hand was Helen but the rod
To scourge a people that, in unknown wise,
    Had vex'd the far Olympian abode
With secret sin or stinted sacrifice.

           *   *   *

XI.

The days grew into months, and months to years,
    And still the Argive army did delay,
Till folk in Troia half forgot their fears,
    And almost as of old were glad and gay;
    And men and maids on Ida dared to stray,
But Helen dwelt within her inmost room,
    And there from dawning to declining day,
Wrought at the patient marvels of her loom.

XII.

Yet even there in peace she might not be:
    There was a nymph, Œnone, in the hills,
The daughter of a River-God was she,
    Of Cebren,—that the mountain silence fills
    With murmur'd music, for the countless rills
Of Ida meet him, dancing to the plain,—
    Her Paris wooed, yet ignorant of ills,
Among the shepherd's huts, nor wooed in vain.

XIII.

Nay, Summer often found them by the fold
    In these glad days, ere Paris was a king,
And oft the Autumn, in his car of gold,
    Had pass'd them, merry at the vintaging:
    And scarce they felt the breath of the white wing
Of Winter, in the cave where they would lie
    On beds of heather by the fire, till Spring
Should crown them with her buds in passing by.

XIV.

For elbow-deep their flowery bed was strown
    With fragrant leaves and with crush'd asphodel,
And sweetly still the shepherd-pipe made moan,
    And many a tale of Love they had to tell,—
    How Daphnis loved the strange, shy maiden well,
And how she loved him not, and how he died,
    And oak-trees moan'd his dirge, and blossoms fell
Like tears from lindens by the water-side!

XV.

But colder, fleeter than the Winter's wing,
    Time pass'd; and Paris changed, and now no more
Œnone heard him on the mountain sing,
    Not now she met him in the forest hoar.
    Nay, but she knew that on an alien shore
An alien love he sought; yet was she strong
    To live, who deem'd that even as of yore
In days to come might Paris love her long.

XVI.

For dark Œnone from her Father drew
    A power beyond all price; the gift to deal
With wounded men, though now the dreadful dew
    Of Death anoint them, and the secret seal
    Of Fate be set on them; these might she heal;
And thus Œnone trusted still to save
    Her lover at the point of death, and steal
His life from Helen, and the amorous grave.

XVII.

And she had borne, though Paris knew it not,
    A child, fair Corythus, to be her shame,
And still she mused, whenas her heart was hot,
    "He hath no child by that Achaean dame:"
    But when her boy unto his manhood came,
Then sorer yet Œnone did repine,
    And bade him "fare to Ilios, and claim
Thy father's love, and all that should be thine!"

XVIII.

Therewith a golden bodkin from her hair
    She drew, and from a green-tress'd birchen tree
She pluck'd a strip of smooth white bark and fair,
    And many signs and woful graved she,
    A message of the evil things to be.
Then deftly closed the birch-bark, fold on fold,
    And bound the tokens well and cunningly,
Three times and four times, with a thread of gold.

XIX.

"Give these to Argive Helen's hand," she cried:
    And so embraced her child, and with no fear
Beheld him leaping down the mountain-side,
    Like a king's son that goes to hunt the deer,
    Clad softly, and in either hand a spear,
With two swift-footed hounds that follow'd him,
    So leap'd he down the grassy slopes and sheer,
And won the precinct of the forest dim.

XX.

He trod that ancient path his sire had trod,
    Far, far below he saw the sea, the town;
He moved as light as an immortal god,
    For mansions in Olympus gliding down.
    He left the shadow of the forest brown,
And through the shallow waters did he cross,
    And stood, ere twilight fell, within the crown
Of towers, the sacred keep of Ilios.

XXI.

Now folk that mark'd him hasting deem'd that he
    Had come to tell the host was on its way,
As one that from the hills had seen the sea
    Beclouded with the Danaan array,
    So straight to Paris' house with no delay
They led him, and did eagerly await
    Within the forecourt, in the twilight grey,
To hear some certain message of their fate.

XXII.

Now Paris was asleep upon his bed
    Tired with a listless day; but all along
The palace chambers Corythus was led,
    And still he heard a music, shrill and strong,
    That seem'd to clamour of an old-world wrong,
And hearts a long time broken; last they came
    To Helen's bower, the fountain of the song
That cried so loud against an ancient shame.

XXIII.

And Helen fared before a mighty loom,
    And sang, and cast her shuttle wrought of gold,
And forth unto the utmost secret room
    The wave of her wild melody was roll'd;
    And still she fashion'd marvels manifold,
Strange shapes of fish and serpent, bear and swan,
    The loves of the immortal Gods of old,
Wherefrom the peoples of the world began.

XXIV.

Now Helen met the stranger graciously
    With gentle speech, and bade set forth a chair
Well wrought of cedar wood and ivory
    That wise Icmalius had fashion'd fair.
    But when young Corythus had drunk the rare
Wine of the princes, and had broken bread,
    Then Helen took the word, and bade declare
His instant tidings; and he spake and said,

XXV.

"Lady and Queen, I have a secret word,
    And bear a token sent to none but thee,
Also I bring message to my Lord
    That spoken to another may not be."
    Then Helen gave a sign unto her three
Bower-maidens, and they went forth from that place,
    Silent they went; and all forebodingly,
They left the man and woman face to face.

XXVI.

Then from his breast the birchen scroll he took
    And gave to Helen; and she read therein:
"Oh thou that on those hidden runes dost look,
    Hast thou forgotten quite thine ancient sin,
    Thy Lord, thy lofty palace, and thy kin,
Even as thy Love forgets the words he spoke
    The strong oath broken one weak heart to win,
The lips that kiss'd him, and the heart that broke?

XXVII.

"Nay, but methinks thou shalt not quite forget
    The curse wherewith I curse thee till I die;
The tears that on the wood-nymph's cheeks are wet,
    Shall burn thy hateful beauty deathlessly,
    Nor shall God raise up seed to thee; but I
Have borne thy love this messenger: my son,
    Who yet shall make him glad, for Time goes by
And soon shall thine enchantments all be done:

XXVIII.

"Ay, soon 'twixt me and Death must be his choice,
    And little in that hour will Paris care
For thy sweet lips, and for thy singing voice,
    Thine arms of ivory, thy golden hair.
    Nay, me will he embrace, and will not spare,
But bid the folk that hate thee have their joy,
    And give thee to the mountain beasts to tear,
Or burn thy body on a tower of Troy."

XXIX.

Even as she read, by Aphrodite's will
    The cloud roll'd back from Helen's memory:
She saw the city of the rifted hill,
    Fair Lacedaemon, 'neath her mountain high;
    She knew the swift Eurotas running by
To mix his sacred waters with the sea,
    And from the garden close she heard the cry
Of her beloved child, Hermione.

XXX.

Then instantly the horror of her shame
    Fell on her, and she saw the coming years;
Famine, and fire, and plague, and all men's blame,
    The wounds of warriors and the women's fears;
    And through her heart her sorrow smote like spears,
And in her soul she knew the utmost smart
    Of wives left lonely, sires bereaved, the tears
Of maidens desolate, of loves that part.

XXXI.

She drain'd the dregs out of the cup of hate;
    The bitterness of sorrow, shame, and scorn;
Where'er the tongues of mortals curse their fate,
    She saw herself an outcast and forlorn;
    And hating sore the day that she was born,
Down in the dust she cast her golden head,
    There with rent raiment and fair tresses torn,
At feet of Corythus she lay for dead.

XXXII.

But Corythus, beholding her sweet face,
    And her most lovely body lying low,
Had pity on her grief and on her grace,
    Nor heeded now she was his mother's foe,
    But did what might be done to ease her woe,
While, as he thought, with death for life she strove,
    And loosed the necklet 'round her neck of snow,
As who that saw had deem'd, with hands of love.

XXXIII.

And there was one that saw: for Paris woke
    Half-deeming and half-dreaming that the van
Of the great Argive host had scared the folk,
    And down the echoing corridor he ran
    To Helen's bower, and there beheld the man
That kneel'd beside his lady lying there:
    No word he spake, but drove his sword a span
Through Corythus' fair neck and cluster'd hair.

XXXIV.

Then fell fair Corythus, as falls the tower
    An earthquake shaketh from a city's crown,
Or as a tall white fragrant lily-flower
    A child hath in the garden trampled down,
    Or as a pine-tree in the forest brown,
Fell'd by the sea-rovers on mountain lands,
    When they to harry foreign folk are boune,
Taking their own lives in their reckless hands.

XXXV.

But still in Paris did his anger burn,
    And still his sword was lifted up to slay,
When, like a lot leap'd forth of Fate's own urn,
    He mark'd the graven tokens where they lay,
    'Mid Helen's hair in golden disarray,
And looking on them, knew what he had done,
    Knew what dire thing had fallen on that day,
Knew how a father's hand had slain a son.

XXXVI.

Then Paris on his face fell grovelling,
    And the night gather'd, and the silence grew
Within the darkened chamber of the king.
    But Helen rose, and a sad breath she drew,
    And her new woes came back to her anew:
Ah, where is he but knows the bitter pain
    To wake from dreams, and find his sorrow true,
And his ill life returned to him again!

XXXVII.

She needed none to tell her whence it fell,
    The thick red rain upon the marble floor:
She knew that in her bower she might not dwell,
    Alone with her own heart for ever more;
    No sacrifice, no spell, no priestly lore
Could banish quite the melancholy ghost
    Of Corythus; a herald sent before
Them that should die for her, a dreadful host.

XXXVIII.

But slowly Paris raised him from the earth,
    And read her face, and knew that she knew all,
No more her eyes, in tenderness or mirth,
    Should answer his, in bower or in hall.
    Nay, Love had fallen when his child did fall,
The stream Love cannot cross ran 'twixt them red;
    No more was Helen his, whate'er befall,
Not though the Goddess drove her to his bed.

XXXIX.

This word he spake, "the Fates are hard on us"—
    Then bade the women do what must be done
To the fair body of dead Corythus.
    And then he hurl'd into the night alone,
    Wailing unto the spirit of his son,
That somewhere in dark mist and sighing wind
    Must dwell, nor yet to Hades had it won,
Nor quite had left the world of men behind.

XL.

But wild Œnone by the mountain-path
    Saw not her son returning to the wold,
And now was she in fear, and now in wrath
    She cried, "He hath forgot the mountain fold,
    And goes in Ilios with a crown of gold:"
But even then she heard men's axes smite
    Against the beeches slim and ash-trees old,
These ancient trees wherein she did delight.

XLI.

Then she arose and silently as Sleep,
  Unseen she follow'd the slow-rolling wain,
Beneath an ashen sky that 'gan to weep,
  Too heavy laden with the latter rain;
  And all the folk of Troy upon the plain
She found, all gather'd 'round a funeral pyre,
  And thereon lay her son, her darling slain,
The goodly Corythus, her heart's desire!

XLII.

Among the spices and fair robes he lay,
  His arm beneath his head, as though he slept.
For so the Goddess wrought that no decay,
  No loathly thing about his body crept;
  And all the people look'd on him and wept,
And, weeping, Paris lit the pine-wood dry,
  And lo, a rainy wind arose and swept
The flame and fragrance far into the sky.

XLIII.

But when the force of flame was burning low,
  Then did they drench the pyre with ruddy wine,
And the white bones of Corythus bestow
  Within a gold cruse, wrought with many a sign,
  And wrapp'd the cruse about with linen fine
And bare it to the tomb: when, lo, the wild
  Œnone sprang, with burning eyes divine,
And shriek'd unto the slayer of her child:

XLIV.

"Oh Thou, that like a God art sire and slayer,
  That like a God, dost give and take away!
Methinks that even now I hear the prayer
  Thou shalt beseech me with, some later day;
  When all the world to thy dim eyes grow grey,
And thou shalt crave thy healing at my hand,
  Then gladly will I mock, and say thee nay,
And watch thine hours run down like running sand!

XLV.

"Yea, thou shalt die, and leave thy love behind,
    And little shall she love thy memory!
But, oh ye foolish people, deaf and blind,
    What Death is coming on you from the sea?"
    Then all men turned, and lo, upon the lee
Of Tenedos, beneath the driving rain,
    The countless Argive ships were racing free,
The wind and oarsmen speeding them amain.

XLVI.

Then from the barrow and the burial,
    Back like a bursting torrent all men fled
Back to the city and the sacred wall.
    But Paris stood, and lifted not his head.
    Alone he stood, and brooded o'er the dead,
As broods a lion, when a shaft hath flown,
    And through the strong heart of his mate hath sped,
Then will he face the hunters all alone.

XLVII.

But soon the voice of men on the sea-sand
    Came 'round him; and he turned, and gazed, and lo!
The Argive ships were dashing on the strand:
    Then stealthily did Paris bend his bow,
    And on the string he laid a shaft of woe,
And drew it to the point, and aim'd it well.
    Singing it sped, and through a shield did go,
And from his barque Protesilaus fell.

XLVIII.

Half gladdened by the omen, through the plain
    Went Paris to the walls and mighty gate,
And little heeded he that arrowy rain
    The Argive bowmen shower'd in helpless hate.
    Nay; not yet feather'd was the shaft of Fate,
His bane, the gift of mighty Heracles
    To Philoctetes, lying desolate,
Within a far off island of the seas.

BOOK V
THE WAR.

*The war 'round Troy, and how many brave men fell, and
chiefly Sarpedon, Patroclus, Hector, Memnon, and Achilles.
The coming of the Amazon, and the wounding of Paris, and
his death, and concerning the good end that Œnone made.*

I.

For ten long years the Argive leaguer lay
    Round Priam's folk, and wrought them many woes,
While, as a lion crouch'd above his prey,
    The Trojans yet made head against their foes;
    And as the swift sea-water ebbs and flows
Between the Straits of Helle and the main,
    Even so the tide of battle sank and rose,
And fill'd with waifs of war the Ilian plain.

II.

And horse on horse was driven, as wave on wave;
    Like rain upon the deep the arrows fell,
And like the wind, the war-cry of the brave
    Rang out above the battle's ebb and swell,
    And long the tale of slain, and sad to tell;
Yet seem'd the end scarce nearer than of yore
    When nine years pass'd and still the citadel
Frown'd on the Argive huts beside the shore.

III.

And still the watchers on the city's crown
    Afar from sacred Ilios might spy
The flame from many a fallen subject town
    Flare on the starry verges of the sky,
    And still from rich Maeonia came the cry
Of cities sack'd where'er Achilles led.
    Yet none the more men deem'd the end was nigh
While knightly Hector fought unvanquished.

IV.

But ever as each dawn bore grief afar,
    And further back, wax'd Paris glad and gay,
And on the fringes of the cloud of war
    His arrows, like the lightning, still would play;
    Yet fled he Menelaus on a day,
And there had died, but Aphrodite's power
    Him in a golden cloud did safe convey
Within the walls of Helen's fragrant bower.

V.

But she, in longing for her lord and home,
    And scorn of her wild lover, did withdraw
From all men's eyes: but in the night would roam
    Till drowsy watchmen of the city saw
    A shadowy shape that chill'd the night with awe,
Treading the battlements; and like a ghost,
    She stretch'd her lovely arms without a flaw,
In shame and longing, to the Argive host.

VI.

But all day long within her bower she wept,
    Still dreaming of the dames renown'd of old,
Whom hate or love of the Immortals swept
    Within the toils of Ate manifold;
    And most she loved the ancient tales that told
How the great Gods, at length to pity stirr'd,
    Changed Niobe upon the mountains cold,
To a cold stone; and Procne to a bird,

VII.

And Myrrha to an incense-breathing tree;—
    "And ah," she murmur'd, "that the Gods were kind,
And bade the Harpies lay their hands on me,
    And bear me with the currents of the wind
    To the dim end of all things, and the blind
Land where the Ocean turneth in his bed:
    Then should I leave mine evil days behind,
And Sleep should fold his wings above my head."

VIII.

And once she heard a Trojan woman bless
    The fair-haired Menelaus, her good lord,
As brave among brave men, not merciless,
    Not swift to slay the captives of his sword,
    Nor wont was he to win the gold abhorr'd
Of them that sell their captives over sea,
    And Helen sighed, and bless'd her for that word,
"Yet will he ne'er be merciful to me!"

IX.

In no wise found she comfort; to abide
    In Ilios was to dwell with shame and fear,
And if unto the Argive host she hied,
    Then should she die by him that was most dear.
    And still the days dragg'd on with bitter cheer,
Till even the great Gods had little joy,
    So fast their children fell beneath the spear,
Below the windy battlements of Troy.

X.

Yet many a prince of south lands, or of east,
    For dark Cassandra's love came trooping in,
And Priam made them merry at the feast,
    And all night long they dream'd of wars to win,
    And with the morning hurl'd into the din,
And cried their lady's name for battle-cry,
    And won no more than this: for Paris' sin,
By Diomede's or Aias' hand to die.

XI.

But for one hour within the night of woes
    The hope of Troy burn'd steadfast as a star;
When strife among the Argive lords arose,
    And dread Achilles held him from the war;
    Yea, and Apollo from his golden car
And silver bow his shafts of evil sped,
    And all the plain was darken'd, near and far,
With smoke above the pyres of heroes dead.

XII.

And many a time through vapour of that smoke
    The shafts of Troy fell fast; and on the plain
All night the Trojan watch fires burn'd and broke
    Like evil stars athwart a mist of rain.
    And through the arms and blood, and through the slain,
Like wolves among the fragments of the fight,
    Crept spies to slay whoe'er forgat his pain
One hour, and fell on slumber in the night.

XIII.

And once, when wounded chiefs their tents did keep,
    And only Aias might his weapons wield,
Came Hector with his host, and smiting deep,
    Brake bow and spear, brake axe and glaive and shield,
    Bulwark and battlement must rend and yield,
And by the ships he smote the foe and cast
    Fire on the ships; and o'er the stricken field,
The Trojans saw that flame arise at last!

XIV.

But when Achilles saw the soaring flame,
    And knew the ships in peril, suddenly
A change upon his wrathful spirit came,
    Nor will'd he that the Danaans should die:
    But call'd his Myrmidons, and with a cry
They follow'd where, like foam on a sea-wave
    Patroclus' crest was dancing, white and high,
Above the tide that back the Trojans drave.

XV.

But like a rock amid the shifting sands,
    And changing springs, and tumult of the deep,
Sarpedon stood, till 'neath Patroclus' hands,
    Smitten he fell; then Death and gentle Sleep
    Bare him from forth the battle to the steep
Where shines his castle o'er the Lycian dell;
    There hath he burial due, while all folk weep
Around the kindly Prince that loved them well.

XVI.

Not unavenged he fell, nor all alone
    To Hades did his soul indignant fly,
For soon was keen Patroclus overthrown
    By Hector, and the God of archery;
    And Hector stripp'd his shining panoply,
Bright arms Achilles lent: ah! naked then,
    Forgetful wholly of his chivalry,
Patroclus lay, nor heard the strife of men.

XVII.

Then Hector from the war a little space
  Withdrew, and clad him in Achilles' gear,
And braced the gleaming helmet on his face,
  And donn'd the corslet, and that mighty spear
  He grasped—the lance that makes the boldest fear;
And home his comrades bare his arms of gold,
  Those Priam once had worn, his father dear,
But in his father's arms he waxed not old!

XVIII.

Then 'round Patroclus' body, like a tide
  That storms the swollen outlet of a stream
When the winds blow, and the rains fall, and wide
  The river runs, and white the breakers gleam,—
  Trojans and Argives battled till the beam
Of Helios was sinking to the wave,
  And now they near'd the ships: yet few could deem
That arms of Argos might the body save.

XIX.

But even then the tidings sore were borne
  To great Achilles, of Patroclus dead,
And all his goodly raiment hath he torn,
  And cast the dust upon his golden head,
  And many a tear and bitter did he shed.
Ay; there by his own sword had he been slain,
  But swift his Goddess-mother, Thetis, sped
Forth with her lovely sea-nymphs from the main.

XX.

For, as a mother when her young child calls
  Hearkens to that, and hath no other care:
So Thetis, from her green and windless halls
  Rose, at the first word of Achilles' prayer,
  To comfort him, and promise gifts of fair
New armour wrought by an immortal hand;
  Then like a silver cloud she scaled the air,
Where bright the dwellings of Olympus stand.

XXI.

But, as a beacon from a 'leaguer'd town
    Within a sea-girt isle, leaps suddenly,
A cloud by day; but when the sun goes down,
    The tongues of fire flash out, and soar on high,
    To summon warlike men that dwell thereby
And bid them bring a rescue over-seas,—
    So now Athene sent a flame to fly
From brow and temples of Aeacides.

XXII.

Then all unarm'd he sped, and through the throng,
    He pass'd to the dyke's edge, beyond the wall,
Nor leap'd the ranks of fighting men among,
    But shouted clearer than the clarion's call
    When foes on a beleaguer'd city fall.
Three times he cried, and terror fell on these
    That heard him; and the Trojans, one and all,
Fled from that shouting of Aeacides.

XXIII.

Backward the Trojans reel'd in headlong flight,
    Chariots and men, and left their bravest slain;
And the sun fell; hut Troy through all the night
    Watch'd by her fires upon the Ilian plain,
    For Hector did the sacred walls disdain
Of Ilios; nor knew that he should stand
    Ere night return'd, and burial crave in vain,
Unarm'd, forsaken, at Achilles' hand.

XXIV.

But all that night within his chamber high
    Hephaestus made his iron anvils ring;
And, ere the dawn, had wrought a panoply,
    The goodliest ever worn by mortal king.
    This to the Argive camp did Thetis bring,
And when her child had proved it, like the star
    That heralds day, he went forth summoning
The host Achaean to delight of war.

XXV.

And as a mountain torrent leaves its bed,
    And seaward sweeps the toils of men in spate,
Or as a forest-fire, that overhead
    Burns in the boughs, a thing insatiate,
    So raged the fierce Achilles in his hate;
And Xanthus, angry for his Trojans slain,
    Brake forth, while fire and wind made desolate
What war and wave had spared upon the plain.

XXVI.

Now through the fume and vapour of the smoke
    Between the wind's voice and the water's cry,
The battle shouting of the Trojans broke,
    And reached the Ilian walls confusedly,
    But over soon the folk that watch'd might spy
Thin broken bands that fled, avoiding death,
    Yet many a man beneath the spear must die,
Ere by the sacred gateway they drew breath.

XXVII.

And as when fire doth on a forest fall
    And hot winds bear it raging in its flight,
And beechen boughs, and pines are ruin'd all,
    So raged Achilles' anger in that fight;
    And many an empty car, with none to smite
The madden'd horses, o'er the bridge of war
    Was wildly whirled, and many a maid's delight
That day to the red wolves was dearer far.

                 *   *   *

XXVIII.

Some Muse that loved not Troy hath done thee wrong,
    Homer! who whisper'd thee that Hector fled
Thrice 'round the sacred walls he kept so long;
    Nay, when he saw his people vanquished
    Alone he stood for Troy; alone he sped
One moment, to the struggle of the spear,
    And, by the Gods deserted, fell and bled,
A warrior stainless of reproach and fear.

XXIX.

Then all the people from the battlement
    Beheld what dreadful things Achilles wrought,
For on the body his revenge he spent,
    The anger of the high Gods heeding nought,
    To whom was Hector dearest, while he fought,
Of all the Trojan men that were their joy,
    But now no more their favour might be bought
By savour of his hecatombs in Troy.

XXX.

So for twelve days rejoiced the Argive host,
    And now Patroclus hath to Hades won,
But Hector naked lay, and still his ghost
    Must wail where waters of Cocytus run;
    Till Priam did what no man born hath done,
Who dared to pass among the Argive bands,
    And clasp'd the knees of him that slew his son,
And kiss'd his awful homicidal hands.

XXXI.

At such a price was Hector's body sent
    To Ilios, where the women wail'd him shrill;
And Helen's sorrow brake into lament
    As bursts a lake the barriers of a hill,
    For lost, lost, lost was that one friend who still
Stood by her with kind speech and gentle heart,
    The sword of war, pure faith, and steadfast will,
That strove to keep all evil things apart.

*   *   *

XXXII.

And so men buried Hector. But they came,
    The Amazons, from frozen fields afar.
A match for heroes in the dreadful game
    Of spears, the darlings of the God of War,
    Whose coming was to Priam dearer far
Than light to him that is a long while blind,
    When leech's hand hath taen away the bar
That vex'd him, or the healing God is kind;

XXXIII.

And Troy was glad, and with the morning light
    The Amazons went forth to slay and slay;
And wondrously they drave the foe in flight,
    Until the Sun had wander'd half his way;
    But when he stoop'd to twilight and the grey
Hour when men loose the steer beneath the yoke,
    No more Achilles held him from the fray,
But dreadful through the women's ranks he broke.

XXXIV.

Then comes eclipse upon the crescent shield,
    And death on them that bear it, and they fall
One here, one there, about the stricken field,
    As in that art, of Love memorial,
    Which moulders on the holy Carian wall.
Ay, still we see, still love, still pity there
    The warrior-maids, so brave, so god-like tall,
In Time's despite imperishably fair.

XXXV.

But, as a dove that braves a falcon, stood
    Penthesilea, wrath outcasting fear,
Or as a hind, that in the darkling wood
    Withstands a lion for her younglings dear;
    So stood the girl before Achilles' spear;
In vain, for singing from his hand it sped,
    And crash'd through shield and breastplate till the sheer
Cold bronze drank blood, and down the queen fell dead.

XXXVI.

Then from her locks the helm Achilles tore
    And boasted o'er the slain; but lo, the face
Of her thus lying in the dust and gore
    Seem'd lovelier than is the maiden grace
    Of Artemis, when weary from the chase,
She sleepeth in a haunted dell unknown.
    And all the Argives marvell'd for a space,
But most Achilles made a heavy moan:

XXXVII.

And in his heart there came the weary thought
    Of all that was, and all that might have been,
Of all the sorrow that his sword had wrought,
    Of Death that now drew near him: of the green
    Vales of Larissa, where, with such a queen,
With such a love as now his spear had slain,
    He had been happy, who must wind the skein
Of grievous wars, and ne'er be glad again.

XXXVIII.

Yea, now wax'd Fate half weary of her game,
    And had no care but aye to kill and kill,
And many young kings to the battle came,
    And of that joy they quickly had their fill,
    And last came Memnon: and the Trojans still
Took heart, like wearied mariners that see
    (Long toss'd on unknown waves at the winds' will)
Through clouds the gleaming crest of Helike.

XXXIX.

For Memnon was the child of the bright Dawn,
    A Goddess wedded to a mortal king,
Who dwells for ever on the shores withdrawn
    That border on the land of sun-rising;
    And he was nurtured nigh the sacred spring
That is the hidden fountain of all seas,
    By them that in the Gods' own garden sing,
The lily-maidens call'd Hesperides.

XL.

But him the child of Thetis in the fight
    Met on a windy winter day, when high
The dust was whirled, and wrapp'd them like the night
    That falleth on the mountains stealthily
    When the floods come, and down their courses dry
The torrents roar, and lightning flasheth far:
    So rang, so shone their harness terribly
Beneath the blinding thunder-cloud of war.

XLI.

Then the Dawn shudder'd on her golden throne,
    And called unto the West Wind, and he blew
And brake the cloud asunder; and alone
    Achilles stood, but Memnon, smitten through,
    Lay beautiful amid the dreadful dew
Of battle, and a deathless heart was fain
    Of tears, to Gods impossible, that drew
From mortal hearts a little of their pain.

XLII..

But now, their leader slain, the Trojans fled,
    And fierce Achilles drove them in his hate,
Avenging still his dear Patroclus dead,
    Nor knew the hour with his own doom was great,
    Nor trembled, standing in the Scaean gate,
Where ancient prophecy foretold his fall;
    Then suddenly there sped the bolt of Fate,
And smote Achilles by the Ilian wall:

XLIII.

From Paris' bow it sped, and even there,
    Even as he grasp'd the skirts of victory,
Achilles fell, nor any man might dare
    From forth the Trojan gateway to draw nigh;
    But, as the woodmen watch a lion die,
Pierced with the hunter's arrow, nor come near
    Till Death hath veil'd his eyelids utterly,
Even so the Trojans held aloof in fear.

XLIV.

But there his fellows on his wondrous shield
    Laid the fair body of Achilles slain,
And sadly bare him through the trampled field,
    And lo! the deathless maidens of the main
    Rose up, with Thetis, from the windy plain,
And 'round the dead man beautiful they cried,
    Lamenting, and with melancholy strain
The sweet-voiced Muses mournfully replied.

XLV.

Yea, Muses and Sea-maidens sang his dirge,
　　And mightily the chant arose and shrill,
And wondrous echoes answer'd from the surge
　　Of the grey sea, and from the holy hill
　　Of Ida; and the heavy clouds and chill
Were gathering like mourners, sad and slow,
　　And Zeus did thunder mightily, and fill
The dells and glades of Ida deep with snow.

XLVI.

Now Paris was not sated with the fame
　　And rich reward Troy gave his archery;
But o'er the wine he boasted that the game
　　That very night he deem'd to win, or die;
　　"For scarce their watch the tempest will defy,"
He said, "and all undream'd of might we go,
　　And fall upon the Argives where they lie,
Unseen, unheard, amid the silent snow."

XLVII.

So, flush'd with wine, and clad in raiment white
　　Above their mail, the young men follow'd him,
Their guide a fading camp-fire in the night,
　　And the sea's moaning in the distance dim.
　　And still with eddying snow the air did swim,
And darkly did they wend they knew not where,
　　White in that cursed night: an army grim,
'Wilder'd with wine, and blind with whirling air.

XLVIII.

There was an outcast in the Argive host,
　　One Philoctetes; whom Odysseus' wile,
(For, save he help'd, the Leaguer all was lost,)
　　Drew from his lair within the Lemnian isle.
　　But him the people, as a leper vile,
Hated, and drave to a lone hut afar,
　　For wounded sore was he, and many a while
His cries would wake the host foredone with war.

XLIX.

Now Philoctetes was an archer wight;
    But in his quiver had he little store
Of arrows tipp'd with bronze, and feather'd bright;
    Nay, his were blue with mould, and fretted o'er
    With many a spell Melampus wrought of yore,
Singing above his task a song of bane;
    And they were venom'd with the Centaur's gore,
And tipp'd with bones of men a long while slain.

L.

This wretch for very pain might seldom sleep,
    And that night slept not: in the moaning blast
He deem'd the dead about his hut did creep,
    And silently he rose, and 'round him cast
    His raiment foul, and from the door he pass'd,
And peer'd into the night, and soothly heard
    A whisper'd voice; then gripp'd his arrows fast
And strung his bow, and cried a bitter word:

LI.

"Art thou a gibbering ghost with war outworn,
    And thy faint life in Hades not begun?
Art thou a man that holdst my grief in scorn,
    And yet dost live, and look upon the sun?
    If man,—methinks thy pleasant days are done,
And thou shalt writhe in torment worse than mine;
    If ghost,—new pain in Hades hast thou won,
And there with double woe shalt surely pine."

LII.

He spake, and drew the string, and sent a shaft
    At venture through the midnight and the snow,
A little while he listen'd, then he laugh'd
    Within himself, a dreadful laugh and low;
    For over well the answer did he know
That midnight gave his message, the sharp cry
    And armour rattling on a fallen foe
That now was learning what it is to die.

LIII.

Then Philoctetes crawl'd into his den
    And hugg'd himself against the bitter cold,
While 'round their leader came the Trojan men
    And bound his wound, and bare him o'er the wold,
    Back to the lights of Ilios; but the gold
Of Dawn was breaking on the mountains white,
    Or ere they won within the guarded fold,
Long 'wilder'd in the tempest and the night.

LIV.

And through the gate, and through the silent street,
    And houses where men dream'd of war no more,
The bearers wander'd with their weary feet,
    And Paris to his high-roof'd house they bore.
    But vainly leeches on his wound did pore,
And vain was Argive Helen's magic song,
    Ah, vain her healing hands, and all her lore,
To help the life that wrought her endless wrong.

LV.

Slow pass'd the fever'd hours, until the grey
    Cold light was paling, and a sullen glow
Of livid yellow crown'd the dying day,
    And brooded on the wastes of mournful snow.
    Then Paris whisper'd faintly, "I must go
And face that wild wood-maiden of the hill;
    For none but she can win from overthrow
Troy's life, and mine that guards it, if she will."

LVI.

So through the dumb white meadows, deep with snow,
    They bore him on a pallet shrouded white,
And sore they dreaded lest an ambush'd foe
    Should hear him moan, or mark the moving light
    That waved before their footsteps in the night;
And much they joy'd when Ida's knees were won,
    And 'neath the pines upon an upland height,
They watch'd the star that heraldeth the sun.

LVII.

For under woven branches of the pine,
 The soft dry needles like a carpet spread,
And high above the arching boughs did shine
 In frosty fret of silver, that the red
 New dawn fired into gold-work overhead:
Within that vale where Paris oft had been
 With fair Œnone, ere the hills he fled
To be the sinful lover of a Queen.

LVIII.

Not here they found Œnone: "Nay, not here,"
 Said Paris, faint and low, "shall she be found;
Nay, bear me up the mountain, where the drear
 Winds walk for ever on a haunted ground.
 Methinks I hear her sighing in their sound;
Or some God calls me there, a dying man.
 Perchance my latest journeying is bound
Back where the sorrow of my life began."

LIX.

They reach'd the gateway of that highest glen
 And halted, wond'ring what the end should be;
But Paris whisper'd Helen, while his men
 Fell back: "Here judged I Gods, here shalt thou see
 What judgment mine old love will pass on me.
But hide thee here; thou soon the end shalt know,
 Whether the Gods at length will set thee free
From that old net they wove so long ago."

LX.

Ah, there with wide snows 'round her like a pall,
 Œnone crouch'd in sable robes; as still
As Winter brooding o'er the Summer's fall,
 Or Niobe upon her haunted hill,
 A woman changed to stone by grief, where chill
The rain-drops fall like tears, and the wind sighs:
 And Paris deem'd he saw a deadly will
Unmoved in wild Œnone's frozen eyes.

LXI.

"Nay, prayer to her were vain as prayer to Fate,"
    He murmur'd, almost glad that it was so,
Like some sick man that need no longer wait,
    But his pain lulls as Death draws near his woe.
    And Paris beckon'd to his men, and slow
They bore him dying from that fatal place,
    And did not turn again, and did not know
The soft repentance on Œnone's face.

LXII.

But Paris spake to Helen: "Long ago,
    Dear, we were glad, who never more shall be
Together, where the west winds fainter blow
    Round that Elysian island of the sea,
    Where Zeus from evil days shall set thee free.
Nay, kiss me once, it is a weary while,
    Ten weary years since thou hast smiled on me,
But, Helen, say good-bye, with thine old smile!"

LXIII.

And as the dying sunset through the rain
    Will flush with rosy glow a mountain height,
Even so, at his last smile, a blush again
    Pass'd over Helen's face, so changed and white;
    And through her tears she smiled, his last delight,
The last of pleasant life he knew, for grey
    The veil of darkness gather'd, and the night
Closed o'er his head, and Paris pass'd away.

LXIV.

Then for one hour in Helen's heart re-born,
    Awoke the fatal love that was of old,
Ere she knew all, and the cold cheeks outworn,
    She kiss'd, she kiss'd the hair of wasted gold,
    The hands that ne'er her body should enfold;
Then slow she follow'd where the bearers led,
    Follow'd dead Paris through the frozen wold
Back to the town where all men wish'd her dead.

LXV.

Perchance it was a sin, I know not, this!
    Howe'er it be, she had a woman's heart,
And not without a tear, without a kiss,
    Without some strange new birth of the old smart,
    From her old love of the brief days could part
For ever; though the dead meet, ne'er shall they
    Meet, and be glad by Aphrodite's art,
Whose souls have wander'd each its several way.

*   *   *

LXVI.

And now was come the day when on a pyre
    Men laid fair Paris, in a broider'd pall,
And fragrant spices cast into the fire,
    And 'round the flame slew many an Argive thrall.
    When, like a ghost, there came among them all,
A woman, once beheld by them of yore,
    When first through storm and driving rain the tall
Black ships of Argos dash'd upon the shore.

LXVII.

Not now in wrath Œnone came; but fair
    Like a young bride when nigh her bliss she knows,
And in the soft night of her fallen hair
    Shone flowers like stars, more white than Ida's snows,
    And scarce men dared to look on her, of those
The pyre that guarded; suddenly she came,
    And sprang upon the pyre, and shrill arose
Her song of death, like incense through the flame.

LXVIII.

And still the song, and still the flame went up,
    But when the flame wax'd fierce, the singing died;
And soon with red wine from a golden cup
    Priests drench'd the pyre; but no man might divide
    The ashes of the Bridegroom from the Bride.
Nay, they were wedded, and at rest again,
    As in those old days on the mountain-side,
Before the promise of their youth was vain.

BOOK VI

THE SACK OF TROY.
THE RETURN OF HELEN.

The sack of Troy, and of how Menelaus would have let them
stone Helen, but Aphrodite saved her, and made them
at one again, and how they came home to Lacedaemon,
and of their translation to Elysium.

I.

There came a day, when Trojan spies beheld
   How, o'er the Argive leaguer, all the air
Was pure of smoke, no battle-din there swell'd,
   Nor any clarion-call was sounding there!
   Yea, of the serried ships the strand was bare,
And sea and shore were still, as long ago
   When Ilios knew not Helen, and the fair
Sweet face that makes immortal all her woe.

II.

So for a space the watchers on the wall
   Were silent, wond'ring what these things might mean.
But, at the last, sent messengers to call
   Priam, and all the elders, and the lean
   Remnant of goodly chiefs, that once had been
The shield and stay of Ilios, and her joy,
   Nor yet despair'd, but trusted Gods unseen,
And cast their spears, and shed their blood for Troy.

III.

They came, the more part grey, grown early old,
   In war and plague; but with them was the young
Coroebus, that but late had left the fold
   And flocks of sheep Maeonian hills among,
   And valiantly his lot with Priam flung,
For love of a lost cause and a fair face,—
   The eyes that once the God of Pytho sung,
That now look'd darkly to the slaughter-place.

IV.

Now while the elders kept their long debate,
   Coroebus stole unheeded to his band,
And led a handful by a postern gate
   Across the plain, across the barren land
   Where once the happy vines were wont to stand,
And 'mid the clusters once did maidens sing,—
   But now the plain was waste on every hand,
Though here and there a flower would breathe of Spring.

V.

So swift across the trampled battle-field
　　Unchallenged still, but wary, did they pass,
By many a broken spear or shatter'd shield
　　That in Fate's hour appointed faithless was:
　　Only the heron cried from the morass
By Xanthus' side, and ravens, and the grey
　　Wolves left their feasting in the tangled grass,
Grudging; and loiter'd, nor fled far away.

VI.

There lurk'd no spears in the high river-banks,
　　No ambush by the cairns of men outworn,
But empty stood the huts, in dismal ranks,
　　Where men through all these many years had borne
　　Fierce summer, and the biting winter's scorn;
And here a sword was left, and there a bow,
　　But ruinous seem'd all things and forlorn,
As in some camp forsaken long ago.

VII.

Gorged wolves crept 'round the altars, and did eat
　　The flesh of victims that the priests had slain,
And wild dogs fought above the sacred meat
　　Late offer'd to the deathless Gods in vain,
　　By men that, for reward of all their pain,
Must haul the ropes, and weary at the oar,
　　Or, drowning, clutch at foam amid the main,
Nor win their haven on the Argive shore.

VIII.

Not long the young men marvell'd at the sight,
　　But grasping one a sword, and one the spear
Aias, or Tydeus' son, had borne in fight,
　　They sped, and fill'd the town with merry cheer,
　　For folk were quick the happy news to hear,
And pour'd through all the gates into the plain,
　　Rejoicing as they wander'd far and near,
O'er the long Argive toils endured in vain.

IX.

Ah, sweet it was, without the city walls,
  To hear the doves coo, and the finches sing;
Ah, sweet, to twine their true-love's coronals
  Of woven wind-flowers, and each fragrant thing
  That blossoms in the footsteps of the spring;
And sweet, to lie, forgetful of their grief,
  Where violets trail by waters wandering,
And the wild fig-tree putteth forth his leaf!

X.

Now while they wander'd as they would, they found
  A wondrous thing: a marvel of man's skill,
That stood within a vale of hollow ground,
  And bulk'd scarce smaller than the bitter-hill,—
  The common barrow that the dead men fill
Who died in the long leaguer,—not of earth,
  Was this new portent, but of tree, and still
The Trojans stood, and marvell'd 'mid their mirth.

XI.

Ay, much they wonder'd what this thing might be,
  Shaped like a Horse it was; and many a stain
There show'd upon the mighty beams of tree,
  For some with fire were blacken'd, some with rain
  Were dank and dark amid white planks of plane,
New cut among the trees that now were few
  On wasted Ida; but men gazed in vain,
Nor truth thereof for all their searching knew.

XII.

At length they deem'd it was a sacred thing,
  Vow'd to Poseidon, monarch of the deep,
And that herewith the Argives pray'd the King
  Of wind and wave to lull the seas to sleep;
  So this, they cried, within the sacred keep
Of Troy must rest, memorial of the war;
  And sturdily they haled it up the steep,
And dragg'd the monster to their walls afar.

XIII.

All day they wrought: and children crown'd with flowers
    Laid light hands on the ropes; old men would ply
Their feeble force; so through the merry hours
    They toil'd, midst laughter and sweet minstrelsy,
    And late they drew the great Horse to the high
Crest of the hill, and wide the tall gates swang;
    But thrice, for all their force, it stood thereby
Unmoved, and thrice like smitten armour rang.

XIV.

Natheless they wrought their will; then altar fires
    The Trojans built, and did the Gods implore
To grant fulfilment of all glad desires.
    But from the cups the wine they might not pour,
    The flesh upon the spits did writhe and roar,
The smoke grew red as blood, and many a limb
    Of victims leap'd upon the temple floor,
Trembling; and groans amid the chapels dim

XV.

Rang low, and from the fair Gods' images
    And from their eyes, dropp'd sweat and many a tear;
The walls with blood were dripping, and on these
    That sacrificed, came horror and great fear;
    The holy laurels to Apollo dear
Beside his temple faded suddenly,
    And wild wolves from the mountains drew anear,
And ravens through the temples seem'd to fly.

XVI.

Yet still the men of Troy were glad at heart,
    And o'er strange meat they revell'd, like folk fey,
Though each would shudder if he glanced apart,
    For 'round their knees the mists were gather'd grey,
    Like shrouds on men that Hell-ward take their way;
But merrily withal they feasted thus,
    And laugh'd with crooked lips, and oft would say
Some evil-sounding word and ominous.

XVII.

And Hecuba among her children spake,
   "Let each man choose the meat he liketh best,
For bread no more together shall we break.
   Nay, soon from all my labour must I rest,
   But eat ye well, and drink the red wine, lest
Ye blame my house-wifery among men dead."
   And all they took her saying for a jest,
And sweetly did they laugh at that she said.

XVIII.

Then, like a raven on the of night,
   The wild Cassandra flitted far and near,
Still crying, "Gather, gather for the fight,
   And brace the helmet on, and grasp the spear,
   For lo, the legions of the Night are here!"
So shriek'd the dreadful prophetess divine.
   But all men mock'd, and were of merry cheer;
Safe as the Gods they deem'd them, o'er their wine.

XIX.

For now with minstrelsy the air was sweet,
   The soft spring air, and thick with incense smoke;
And bands of happy dancers down the street
   Flew from the flower-crown'd doors, and wheel'd, and broke;
   And loving words the youths and maidens spoke,
For Aphrodite did their hearts beguile,
   As when beneath grey cavern or green oak
The shepherd men and maidens meet and smile.

XX.

No guard they set, for truly to them all
   Did Love and slumber seem exceeding good;
There was no watch by open gate nor wall,
   No sentinel by Pallas' image stood;
   But silence grew, as in an autumn wood
When tempests die, and the vex'd boughs have ease,
   And wind and sunlight fade, and soft the mood
Of sacred twilight falls upon the trees.

XXI.

Then the stars cross'd the zenith, and there came
    On Troy that hour when slumber is most deep,
But any man that watch'd had seen a flame
    Spring from the tall crest of the Trojan keep;
    While from the belly of the Horse did leap
Men arm'd, and to the gates went stealthily,
    While up the rocky way to Ilios creep
The Argives, new return'd across the sea.

XXII.

Now when the silence broke, and in that hour
    When first the dawn of war was blazing red,
There came a light in Helen's fragrant bower,
    As on that evil night before she fled
    From Lacedaemon and her marriage bed;
And Helen in great fear lay still and cold,
    For Aphrodite stood above her head,
And spake in that sweet voice she knew of old:

XXIII.

"Beloved one that dost not love me, wake!
    Helen, the night is over, the dawn is near,
And safely shalt thou fare with me, and take
    Thy way through fire and blood, and have no fear:
    A little hour, and ended is the drear
Tale of thy sorrow and thy wandering.
    Nay, long hast thou to live in happy cheer,
By fair Eurotas, with thy lord, the King."

XXIV.

Then Helen rose, and in a cloud of gold,
    Unseen amid the vapour of the fire,
Did Aphrodite veil her, fold on fold;
    And through the darkness, throng'd with faces dire,
    And o'er men's bodies fallen in a mire
Of new spilt blood and wine, the twain did go
    Where Lust and Hate were mingled in desire,
And dreams and death were blended in one woe.

XXV.

Fire and the foe were masters now: the sky
    Flared like the dawn of that last day of all,
When men for pity to the sea shall cry,
    And vainly on the mountain tops shall call
    To fall and end the horror in their fall;
And through the vapour dreadful things saw they,
    The maidens leaping from the city wall,
The sleeping children murder'd where they lay.

XXVI.

Yea, cries like those that make the hills of Hell
    Ring and re-echo, sounded through the night,
The screams of burning horses, and the yell
    Of young men leaping naked into fight,
    And shrill the women shriek'd, as in their flight
Shriek the wild cranes, when overhead they spy
    Between the dusky cloud-land and the bright
Blue air, an eagle stooping from the sky.

XXVII.

And now the red glare of the burning shone
    On deeds so dire the pure Gods might not bear,
Save Ares only, long to look thereon,
    But with a cloud they darken'd all the air.
    And, even then, within the temple fair
Of chaste Athene, did Cassandra cower,
    And cried aloud an unavailing prayer;
For Aias was the master in that hour.

XXVIII.

Man's lust won what a God's love might not win,
    And heroes trembled, and the temple floor
Shook, when one cry went up into the din,
    And shamed the night to silence; then the roar
    Of war and fire wax'd great as heretofore,
Till each roof fell, and every palace gate
    Was shatter'd, and the King's blood shed; nor more
Remain'd to do, for Troy was desolate.

XXIX.

Then dawn drew near, and changed to clouds of rose
    The dreadful smoke that clung to Ida's head;
But Ilios was ashes, and the foes
    Had left the embers and the plunder'd dead;
    And down the steep they drove the prey, and sped
Back to the swift ships, with a captive train,—
    While Menelaus, slow, with drooping head,
Follow'd, like one lamenting, through the plain.

XXX.

Where death might seem the surest, by the gate
    Of Priam, where the spears raged, and the tall
Towers on the foe were falling, sought he fate
    To look on Helen once, and then to fall,
    Nor see with living eyes the end of all,
What time the host their vengeance should fulfil,
    And cast her from the cliff below the wall,
Or burn her body on the windy hill.

XXXI.

But Helen found he never, where the flame
    Sprang to the roofs, and Helen ne'er he found
Where flock'd the wretched women in their shame
    The helpless altars of the Gods around,
    Nor lurk'd she in deep chambers underground,
Where the priests trembled o'er their hidden gold,
    Nor where the armed feet of foes resound
In shrines to silence consecrate of old.

XXXII.

So wounded to his hut and wearily
    Came Menelaus; and he bow'd his head
Beneath the lintel neither fair nor high;
    And, lo! Queen Helen lay upon his bed,
    Flush'd like a child in sleep, and rosy-red,
And at his footstep did she wake and smile,
    And spake: "My lord, how hath thy hunting sped,
Methinks that I have slept a weary while!"

XXXIII.

For Aphrodite made the past unknown
　　To Helen, as of old, when in the dew
Of that fair dawn the net was 'round her thrown:
　　Nay, now no memory of Troy brake through
　　The mist that veil'd from her sweet eyes and blue
The dreadful days and deeds all over-past,
　　And gladly did she greet her lord anew,
And gladly would her arms have 'round him cast.

XXXIV.

Then leap'd she up in terror, for he stood
　　Before her, like a lion of the wild,
His rusted armour all bestain'd with blood,
　　His mighty hands with blood of men defiled,
　　And strange was all she saw: the spears, the piled
Raw skins of slaughter'd beasts with many a stain;
　　And low he spake, and bitterly he smiled,
"The hunt is ended, and the spoil is ta'en."

XXXV.

No more he spake; for certainly he deem'd
　　That Aphrodite brought her to that place,
And that of her loved archer Helen dream'd,
　　Of Paris; at that thought the mood of grace
　　Died in him, and he hated her fair face,
And bound her hard, not slacking for her tears;
　　Then silently departed for a space,
To seek the ruthless counsel of his peers.

XXXVI.

Now all the Kings were feasting in much joy,
　　Seated or couch'd upon the carpets fair
That late had strown the palace floors of Troy,
　　And lovely Trojan ladies served them there,
　　And meat from off the spits young princes bare;
But Menelaus burst among them all,
　　Strange, 'mid their revelry, and did not spare,
But bade the Kings a sudden council call.

XXXVII.

To mar their feast the Kings had little will,
    Yet did they as he bade, in grudging wise,
And heralds call'd the host unto the hill
    Heap'd of sharp stones, where ancient Ilus lies.
    And forth the people flock'd, as throng'd as flies
That buzz about the milking-pails in spring,
    When life awakens under April skies,
And birds from dawning into twilight sing.

XXXVIII.

Then Helen through the camp was driven and thrust,
    Till even the Trojan women cried in glee,
"Ah, where is she in whom thou put'st thy trust,
    The Queen of love and laughter, where is she?
    Behold the last gift that she giveth thee,
Thou of the many loves! to die alone,
    And 'round thy flesh for robes of price to be
The cold close-clinging raiment of sharp stone."

XXXIX.

Ah, slowly through that trodden field and bare
    They pass'd, where scarce the daffodil might spring,
For war had wasted all, but in the air
    High overhead the mounting lark did sing;
    Then all the army gather'd in a ring
Round Helen, 'round their torment, trapp'd at last,
    And many took up mighty stones to fling
From shards and flints on Ilus' barrow cast.

XL.

Then Menelaus to the people spoke,
    And swift his wing'd words came as whirling snow,
"Oh ye that overlong have borne the yoke,
    Behold the very fountain of your woe!
    For her ye left your dear homes long ago,
On Argive valley or Boeotian plain;
    But now the black ships rot from stern to prow,
Who knows if ye shall see your own again?

XLI.

"Ay, and if home ye win, ye yet may find,
　　Ye that the winds waft, and the waters bear
To Argos! ye are quite gone out of mind;
　　Your fathers, dear and old, dishonour'd there;
　　Your children deem you dead, and will not share
Their lands with you; on mainland or on isle,
　　Strange men are wooing now the women fair,
And love doth lightly woman's heart beguile.

XLII.

"These sorrows hath this woman wrought alone:
　　So fall upon her straightway that she die,
And clothe her beauty in a cloak of stone!"
　　He spake, and truly deem'd to hear her cry
　　And see the sharp flints straight and deadly fly;
But each man stood and mused on Helen's face,
　　And her undream'd-of beauty, brought so nigh
On that bleak plain, within that ruin'd place.

LXIII.

And as in far off days that were to be,
　　The sense of their own sin did men constrain,
That they must leave the sinful woman free
　　Who, by their law, had verily been slain,
　　So Helen's beauty made their anger vain,
And one by one his gather'd flints let fall;
　　And like men shamed they stole across the plain,
Back to the swift ships and their festival.

XLIV.

But Menelaus look'd on her and said,
　　"Hath no man then condemn'd thee,—is there none
To shed thy blood for all that thou hast shed,
　　To wreak on thee the wrongs that thou hast done.
　　Nay, as mine own soul liveth, there is one
That will not set thy barren beauty free,
　　But slay thee to Poseidon and the Sun
Before a ship Achaian takes the sea!"

XLV.

Therewith he drew his sharp sword from his thigh
    As one intent to slay her: but behold,
A sudden marvel shone across the sky!
    A cloud of rosy fire, a flood of gold,
    And Aphrodite came from forth the fold
Of wondrous mist, and sudden at her feet
    Lotus and crocus on the trampled wold
Brake, and the slender hyacinth was sweet.

XLVI.

Then fell the point that never bloodless fell
    When spear bit harness in the battle din,
For Aphrodite spake, and like a spell
    Wrought her sweet voice persuasive, till within
    His heart there lived no memory of sin,
No thirst for vengeance more, but all grew plain,
    And wrath was molten in desire to win
The golden heart of Helen once again.

XLVII.

Then Aphrodite vanish'd as the day
    Passes, and leaves the darkling earth behind;
And overhead the April sky was grey,
    But Helen's arms about her lord were twined,
    And his 'round her as clingingly and kind,
As when sweet vines and ivy in the spring
    Join their glad leaves, nor tempests may unbind
The woven boughs, so lovingly they cling.

*   *   *

XLVIII.

Noon long was over-past, but sacred night
    Beheld them not upon the Ilian shore;
Nay, for about the waning of the light
    Their swift ships wander'd on the waters hoar,
    Nor stay'd they the Olympians to adore,
So eagerly they left that cursed land,
    But many a toil, and tempests great and sore,
Befell them ere they won the Argive strand.

XLIX.

To Cyprus and Phoenicia wandering
　　They came, and many a ship, and many a man
They lost, and perish'd many a precious thing
　　While bare before the stormy North they ran,
　　And further far than when their quest began
From Argos did they seem,—a weary while,—
　　Becalm'd in sultry seas Egyptian,
A long day's voyage from the mouths of Nile.

L.

But there the Gods had pity on them, and there
　　The ancient Proteus taught them how to flee
From that so distant deep,—the fowls of air
　　Scarce in one year can measure out that sea;
　　Yet first within Aegyptus must they be,
And hecatombs must offer,—quickly then
　　The Gods abated of their jealousy,
Wherewith they scourge the negligence of men.

LI.

And strong and fair the south wind blew, and fleet
　　Their voyaging, so merrily they fled
To win that haven where the waters sweet
　　Of clear Eurotas with the brine are wed,
　　And swift their chariots and their horses sped
To pleasant Lacedaemon, lying low
　　Grey in the shade of sunset, but the head
Of tall Taygetus like fire did glow.

LII.

And what but this is sweet: at last to win
　　The fields of home, that change not while we change;
To hear the birds their ancient song begin;
　　To wander by the well-loved streams that range
　　Where not one pool, one moss-clad stone is strange,
Nor seem we older than long years ago,
　　Though now beneath the grey roof of the grange
The children dwell of them we used to know?

LIII.

Came there no trouble in the later days
    To mar the life of Helen, when the old
Crowns and dominions perish'd, and the blaze
    Lit by returning Heraclidae roll'd
    Through every vale and every happy fold
Of all the Argive land? Nay, peacefully
    Did Menelaus and the Queen behold
The counted years of mortal life go by.

LIV.

"Death ends all tales," but this he endeth not;
    They grew not grey within the valley fair
Of hollow Lacedaemon, but were brought
    To Rhadamanthus of the golden hair,
    Beyond the wide world's end; ah never there
Comes storm nor snow; all grief is left behind,
    And men immortal, in enchanted air,
Breathe the cool current of the Western wind.

LV.

But Helen was a Saint in Heathendom,
    A kinder Aphrodite; without fear
Maidens and lovers to her shrine would come
    In fair Therapnae, by the waters clear
    Of swift Eurotas; gently did she hear
All prayers of love, and not unheeded came
    The broken supplication, and the tear
Of man or maiden overweigh'd with shame.

LVI.

O'er Helen's shrine the grass is growing green,
    In desolate Therapnae; none the less
Her sweet face now unworshipp'd and unseen
    Abides the symbol of all loveliness,
    Of Beauty ever stainless in the stress
Of warring lusts and fears;—and still divine,
    Still ready with immortal peace to bless
Them that with pure hearts worship at her shrine.

NOTE

In this story in rhyme of the fortunes of Helen, the theory that she was an unwilling victim of the Gods has been preferred. Many of the descriptions of manners are versified from the Iliad and the Odyssey. The description of the events after the death of Hector, and the account of the sack of Troy, is chiefly borrowed from Quintus Smyrnaeus.

The character and history of Helen of Troy have been conceived of in very different ways by poets and mythologists. In attempting to trace the chief current of ancient traditions about Helen, we cannot really get further back than the Homeric poems, the Iliad and Odyssey. Philological conjecture may assure us that Helen, like most of the characters of old romance, is "merely the Dawn," or Light, or some other bright being carried away by Paris, who represents Night, or Winter, or the Cloud, or some other power of darkness. Without discussing these ideas, it may be said that the Greek poets (at all events before allegorical explanations of mythology came in, about five hundred years before Christ) regarded Helen simply as a woman of wonderful beauty. Homer was not thinking of the Dawn, or the Cloud when he described Helen among the Elders on the Ilian walls, or repeated her lament over the dead body of Hector. The Homeric poems are our oldest literary documents about Helen, but it is probable enough that the poet has modified and purified more ancient traditions which still survive in various fragments of Greek legend. In Homer Helen is always the daughter of Zeus. Isocrates tells us ("Helena," 211 b) that "while many of the demigods were children of Zeus, he thought the paternity of none of his daughters worth claiming, save that of Helen only." In Homer, then, Helen is the daughter of Zeus, but Homer says nothing of the famous legend which makes Zeus assume the form of a swan to woo the mother of Helen. Unhomeric as this myth is, we may regard it as extremely ancient. Very similar tales of pursuit and metamorphosis, for amatory or other purposes, among the old legends of Wales, and in the "Arabian Nights," as well as in the myths of Australians and Red Indians. Again, the belief that different families of mankind descend from animals, as from the Swan, or from gods in the shape of animals, is found in every quarter of the world, and among the rudest races. Many Australian natives of today claim descent, like the royal house of Sparta, from the Swan. The Greek myths hesitated as to whether Nemesis or Leda was the bride of the Swan. Homer only mentions Leda among "the wives and daughters of mighty men," whose ghosts Odysseus beheld in Hades: "And I saw Leda, the famous bedfellow of Tyndareus, who bare to Tyndareus two sons, hardy of heart, Castor, tamer of steeds, and the boxer Polydeuces." These heroes Helen, in the Iliad (iii. 238), describes as her mother's sons. Thus, if Homer has any distinct view on the subject, he holds that Leda is the mother of Helen by Zeus, of the Dioscuri by Tyndareus.

Greek ideas as to the character of Helen varied with the various moods of Greek literature. Homer's own ideas about his heroine are probably best expressed in the words with which Priam greets her as she appears among the assembled elders, who are watching the Argive heroes from the wall of Troy:—"In nowise, dear child, do I blame thee; nay, the Gods are to blame, who have roused against me the woful war of the Achaeans." Homer, like Priam, throws the guilt of Helen on the Gods, but it is not very easy to understand exactly what he means by saying "the Gods are to blame." In the first place, Homer avoids the psychological problems in which modern poetry revels, by attributing almost all changes of the moods of men to divine inspiration. Thus when Achilles, in a famous passage of the first book of the Iliad, puts up his half-drawn sword in the sheath, and does not slay Agamemnon, Homer assigns his repentance to the direct influence of Athene. Again, he says in the Odyssey, about Clytemnestra, that "she would none of the foul deed;" that is of the love of Aegisthus, till "the doom of the Gods bound her to her ruin." So far the same excuse is made for the murderous Clytemnestra as for the amiable Helen. Again, Homer is, in the strictest sense, and in strong contrast to the Greek tragedians and to Virgil, a chivalrous poet. It would probably be impossible to find a passage in which he speaks harshly or censoriously of the conduct of any fair and noble lady. The sordid treachery of Eriphyle, who sold her lord for gold, wins for her the epithet "hateful;" and Achilles, in a moment of strong grief, applies a term of abhorrence to Helen. But Homer is too chivalrous to judge the life of any lady, and only shows the other side of the chivalrous character—its cruelty to persons not of noble birth—in describing the "foul death" of the waiting women of Penelope. "God forbid that I should take these women's lives by a clean death," says Telemachus (Odyssey, xxii. 462). So "about all their necks nooses were cast that they might die by the death most pitiful. And they writhed with their feet for a little space, but for no long while." In trying to understand Homer's estimate of Helen, therefore, we must make allowance for his theory of divine intervention, and for his chivalrous judgment of ladies. But there are two passages in the Iliad which may be taken as indicating Homer's opinion that Helen was literally a victim, an unwilling victim, of

Aphrodite, and that she was carried away by force a captive from Lacedaemon. These passages are in the Iliad, ii. 356, 590. In the former text Nestor says, "let none be eager to return home ere he has couched with a Trojan's wife, and *avenged the longings and sorrows of Helen.*" It is thus that Mr. Gladstone, a notable champion of Helen's, would render this passage, and the same interpretation was favoured by the ancient "Separatists" (Chorizontes), who wished to prove that the Iliad and Odyssey were by different authors; but many authorities prefer to translate "to avenge our labours and sorrows for Helen's sake"—"to avenge all that we have endured in the attempt to win back Helen." Thus the evidence of this passage is ambiguous. The fairer way to seek for Homer's real view of Helen is to examine all the passages in which she occurs. The result will be something like this:—Homer sees in Helen a being of the rarest personal charm and grace of character; a woman who imputes to herself guilt much greater than the real measure of her offence. She is ever gentle except with the Goddess who betrayed her, and the unworthy lover whose lot she is compelled to share. Against them her helpless anger breaks out in flashes of eloquent scorn. Homer was apparently acquainted with the myth of Helen's capture by Theseus, a myth illustrated in the decorations of the coffer of Cypselus. But we first see Helen, the cause of the war, when Menelaus and Paris are about to fight their duel for her sake, in the tenth year of the Leaguer (Iliad, iii. 121). Iris is sent to summon Helen to the walls. She finds Helen in her chamber, weaving at a mighty loom, and embroidering on tapestry the adventures of the siege—the battles of horse-taming Trojans and bronze-clad Achaeans. The message of Iris renews in Helen's heart "a sweet desire for her lord and her own city, and them that begat her;" so, draped in silvery white, Helen goes with her three maidens to the walls. There, above the gate, like some king in the Old Testament, Paris sits among his counsellors, and they are all amazed at Helen's beauty; "no marvel is it that Trojans and Achaeans suffer long and weary toils for such a woman, so wondrous like to the immortal goddesses." Then Priam, assuring Helen that he holds her blameless, bids her name to him her kinsfolk and the other Achaean warriors. In her reply, Helen displays that grace of penitence which is certainly not often found in ancient literature:—"Would that evil death had been my choice, when I followed thy son, and left my bridal bower and my kin, and my daughter dear, and the maidens of like age with me." Agamemnon she calls, "the husband's brother of me shameless; alas, that such an one should be." She names many of the warriors, but misses her brothers Castor and Polydeuces, "own brothers of mine, one mother bare us. Either they followed not from

97

pleasant Lacedaemon, or hither they followed in swift ships, but now they have no heart to go down into the battle for dread of the shame and many reproaches that are mine."

"So spake she, but already the life-giving earth did cover them, there in Lacedaemon, in their own dear country." Menelaus and Paris fought out their duel, the Trojan was discomfited, but was rescued from death and carried to Helen's bower by Aphrodite. Then the Goddess came in disguise to seek Helen on the wall, and force her back into the arms of her defeated lover. Helen turned on the Goddess with an abruptness and a force of sarcasm and invective which seem quite foreign to her gentle nature. "Wilt thou take me further yet to some city of Phrygia or pleasant Maeonia, if there any man is dear to thee . . . Nay, go thyself and sit down by Paris, and forswear the paths of the Gods, but ever lament for him and cherish him, till he make thee his wife, yea, or perchance his slave, but to him will I never go." But this anger of Helen is soon overcome by fear, when the Goddess, in turn, waxes wrathful, and Helen is literally driven by threats—"for the daughter of Zeus was afraid,"—into the arms of Paris. Yet even so she taunts her lover with his cowardice, a cowardice which she never really condones. In the sixth book of the Iliad she has been urging him to return to the war. She then expresses her penitence to Hector, "would that the fury of the wind had borne me afar to the mountains, or the wave of the roaring sea—ere ever these ill deeds were done!" In this passage too, she prophesies that her fortunes will be famous in the songs, good or evil, of men unborn. In the last book of the Iliad we meet Helen once more, as she laments over the dead body of Hector. "'Never, in all the twenty years since I came hither, have I heard from thee one taunt or one evil word: nay, but if any other rebuked me in the halls, any one of my husband's brothers, or of their sisters, or their wives, or the mother of my husband (but the king was ever gentle to me as a father), then wouldst thou restrain them with thy loving kindness and thy gentle speech.' So spake she; weeping."

In the Odyssey, Helen is once more in Lacedaemon, the honoured but still penitent wife of Menelaus. How they became reconciled (an extremely difficult point in the story), there is nothing in Homer to tell us.

Sir John Lubbock has conjectured that in the morals of the heroic age Helen was not really regarded as guilty. She was lawfully married, by "capture," to Paris. Unfortunately for this theory there is abundant proof that, in the heroic age, wives were nominally *bought* for so many cattle, or given as a reward for great services. There is no sign of marriage by capture, and, again, marriage by capture is a savage institution which applies to unmarried women, not to women already wedded, as Helen was to Menelaus. Perhaps the oldest evidence we have for opinion about the later relations of Helen and Menelaus, is derived from Pausanias's (174. AD.) description of the Chest of Cypselus. This ancient coffer, a work of the seventh century, B.C, was still preserved at Olympia, in the time of Pausanias. On one of the bands of cedar or of ivory, was represented (Pausanias, v. 18), "Menelaus with a sword in his hand, rushing on to kill Helen—clearly at the sacking of Ilios." How Menelaus passed from a desire to kill Helen to his absolute complacency in the Odyssey, Homer does not tell us. According to a statement attributed to Stesichorus (635, 554, B.C.?), the army of the Achaeans purposed to stone Helen, but was overawed and compelled to relent by her extraordinary beauty: "when they beheld her, they cast down their stones on the ground." It may be conjectured that the reconciliation followed this futile attempt at punishing a daughter of Zeus. Homer, then, leaves us without information about the adventures of Helen, between the sack of Tiny and the reconciliation with Menelaus. He hints that she was married to Deiphobus, after the death of Paris, and alludes to the tradition that she mimicked the voices of the wives of the heroes, and so nearly tempted them to leave their ambush in the wooden horse. But in the fourth book of the Odyssey, when Telemachus visits Lacedaemon, he finds Helen the honoured wife of Menelaus, rich in the marvellous gifts bestowed on her, in her wanderings from Troy, by the princes of Egypt.

"While yet he pondered these things in his mind and in his heart, Helen came forth from her fragrant vaulted chamber, like Artemis of the golden arrows; and with her came Adraste and set for her the well-wrought chair, and Alcippe bare a rug of soft wool, and Phylo bare a silver basket which Alcandre gave her, the wife of Polybus, who dwelt in Thebes of Egypt, where is the chiefest store of wealth in the houses. He gave two silver baths to Menelaus, and tripods twain, and ten talents of gold. And besides all this, his wife bestowed on Helen lovely gifts; a golden distaff did she give, and a silver basket with wheels beneath, and the rims thereof were finished with gold. This it was that the handmaid Phylo bare and set beside her, filled with dressed yarn, and across it was laid a distaff charged with wool of violet blue. So Helen sat her down in the chair, and beneath was a footstool for the feet." When the host and guests begin to weep the ready tears of the heroic age over the sorrows of the past, and dread of the dim future, Helen comforts them with a magical potion.

"Then Helen, daughter of Zeus, turned to new thoughts. Presently she cast a drug into the wine whereof they drank, a drug to lull all pain and anger, and bring forgetfulness of every sorrow. Whoso should drink a draught thereof, when it is mingled in the bowl, on that day he would let no tear fall down his cheeks, not though his mother and his father died, not though men slew his brother or dear son with the sword before his face, and his own eyes beheld it. Medicines of such virtue and so helpful had the daughter of Zeus, which Polydamna, the wife of Thon, had given her, a woman of Egypt, where Earth the grain-giver yields herbs in greatest plenty, many that are healing in the cup, and many baneful."

So Telemachus was kindly entertained by Helen and Menelaus, and when he left them it was not without a gift. "And Helen stood by the coffers wherein were her robes of curious needlework which she herself had wrought. Then Helen, the fair lady, lifted one and brought it out, the widest and most beautifully embroidered of all, and it shone like a star, and lay far beneath the rest."

Presently, we read, "Helen of the fair face came up with the robe in her hands, and spake: 'Lo! I too give thee this gift, dear child, a memorial of the hands of Helen, for thy bride to wear upon the day of thy desire, even of thy marriage. But meanwhile let it lie with thy mother in her chamber. And may joy go with thee to thy well-builded house, and thine own country.'"

Helen's last words, in Homer, are words of good omen, her prophecy to Telemachus that Odysseus shall return home after long wanderings, and take vengeance on the rovers. We see Helen no more, but Homer does not leave us in doubt as to her later fortunes. He quotes the prophecy which Proteus, the ancient one of the sea, delivered to Menelaus:—

"But thou, Menelaus, son of Zeus, art not ordained to die and meet thy fate in Argos, the pasture-land of horses, but the deathless gods will convey thee to the Elysian plain and the world's end, where is Rhadamanthus of the fair hair, where life is easiest for men. No snow is there, nor yet great storm, nor any rain; but alway ocean sendeth forth the breeze of the shrill West to blow cool on men: yea, for thou hast Helen to wife, and thereby they deem thee to be son of Zeus." We must believe, with Isocrates, that Helen was translated, with her lord, to that field of Elysium, "where falls not hail, or rain, or any snow." This version of the end of Helen's history we have adopted, but many other legends were known in Greece. Pausanias tells us that, in a battle between the Crotoniats and the Locrians, one Leonymus charged the empty space in the Locrian line, which was entrusted to the care of the ghost of Aias. Leonymus was wounded by the invisible spear of the hero, and could not be healed of the hurt. The Delphian oracle bade him seek the Isle of Leuke in the Euxine Sea, where Aias would appear to him, and heal him. When Leonymus returned from Leuke he told how Achilles dwelt there with his ancient comrades, and how he was now wedded to Helen of Troy. Yet the local tradition of Lacedaemon showed the sepulchre of Helen in Therapnae. According to a Rhodian legend (adopted by the author of the "Epic of Hades"), Helen was banished from Sparta by the sons of Menelaus, came wandering to Rhodes, and was there strangled by the servants of the queen Polyxo, who thus avenged the death of her husband at Troy. It is certain, as we learn both from Herodotus (vi. 61) and from Isocrates, that Helen was worshipped in Therapnae. In the days of Ariston the king, a deformed child was daily brought by her nurse to the shrine of Helen. And it is said that, as the nurse was leaving the shrine, a woman appeared unto her, and asked what she bore in her arms, who said, "she bore a child." Then the woman said, "show it to me," which the nurse refused, for the parents of the child had forbidden that she should be seen of any. But the woman straitly commanding that the child should be shown, and the other beholding her eagerness, at length the nurse showed the child, and the woman caressed its face and said, "she shall be the fairest woman in Sparta." And from that day the fashion of its countenance was changed, "and the child became the fairest of all the Spartan women."

It is a characteristic of Greek literature that, with the rise of democracy, the old epic conception of the ancient heroes altered. We can scarcely recognize the Odysseus of Homer in the Odysseus of Sophocles. The kings are regarded by the tragedians with some of the distrust and hatred which the unconstitutional tyrants of Athens had aroused. Just as the later chansons de geste of France, the poems written in an age of feudal opposition to central authority, degraded heroes like Charles, so rhetorical, republican, and sophistical Greece put its quibbles into the lips of Agamemnon and Helen, and slandered the stainless and fearless Patroclus and Achilles.

The Helen of Euripides, in the "Troades," is a pettifogging sophist, who pleads her cause to Menelaus with rhetorical artifice. In the "Helena," again, Euripides quite deserts the Homeric traditions, and adopts the late myths which denied that Helen ever went to Troy. She remained in Egypt, and Achaeans and Trojans fought for a mere shadow, formed by the Gods out of clouds and wind. In the "Cyclops" of Euripides, a satirical drama, the cynical giant is allowed to speak of Helen in a strain of coarse banter. Perhaps the essay of Isocrates on Helen may be regarded as a kind of answer to the attacks of several speakers in the works of the tragedians. Isocrates defends Helen simply on the plea of her beauty: "To Heracles Zeus gave strength, to Helen beauty, which naturally rules over even strength itself." Beauty, he declares, the Gods themselves consider the noblest thing in the world, as the Goddesses showed when they contended for the prize of loveliness. And so marvellous, says Isocrates, was the beauty of Helen, that for her glory Zeus did not spare his beloved son, Sarpedon; and Thetis saw Achilles die, and the Dawn bewailed her Memnon. "Beauty has raised more mortals to immortality than all the other virtues together." And that Helen is now a Goddess, Isocrates proves by the fact that the sacrifices offered to her in Therapnae, are such as are given, not to heroes, but to immortal Gods.

When Rome took up the legends of Greece, she did so in no chivalrous spirit. Few poets are less chivalrous than Virgil; no hero has less of chivalry than his pious and tearful Aeneas. In the second book of the Aeneid, the pious one finds Helen hiding in the shrine of Vesta, and determines to slay "the common curse of Troy and of her own country." There is no glory, he admits, in murdering a woman:—

Extinxisse nefas tamen et sumpsisse merentis
Laudabor poenas, animumqne explesse juvabit
Ultricis flammae, et cineres satiasse meorum.

But Venus appears and rescues the unworthy lover of Dido from the crowning infamy which he contemplates. Hundreds of years later, Helen found a worthier poet in Quintus Smyrnaeus, who in a late age sang the swan-song of Greek epic minstrelsy. It is thus that (in the fourth century A.D.) Quintus describes Helen, as she is led with the captive women of Ilios, to the ships of the Achaeans:—"Now Helen lamented not, but shame dwelt in her dark eyes, and reddened her lovely cheeks, . . . while around her the people marvelled as they beheld the flawless grace and winsome beauty of the woman, and none dared upbraid her with secret taunt or open rebuke. Nay, as she had been a Goddess they beheld her gladly, for dear and desired was she in their sight. And as when their own country appeareth to men long wandering on the sea, and they, being escaped from death and the deep, gladly put forth their hands to greet their own native place; even so all the Danaans were glad at the sight of her, and had no more memory of all their woful toil, and the din of war: such a spirit did Cytherea put into their hearts, out of favour to fair Helen and father Zeus." Thus Quintus makes amends for the trivial verses in which Coluthus describes the flight of a frivolous Helen with an effeminate Paris.

To follow the fortunes of Helen through the middle ages would demand much space and considerable research. The poets who read Dares Phrygius believed, with the scholar of Dr. Faustus, that "Helen of Greece was the admirablest lady that ever lived." When English poetry first found the secret of perfect music, her sweetest numbers were offered by Marlowe at the shrine of Helen. The speech of Faustus is almost too hackneyed to be quoted, and altogether too beautiful to be omitted:—

Was this the face that launched a thousand ships,
And burnt the topless towers of Ilium!
Sweet Helen, make me immortal with a kiss.
Her lips suck forth my soul! see where it flies;
Come, Helen, come, give me my soul again;
Here will I dwell, for heaven is in those lips,
And all is dross that is not Helena.

        *   *   *

Oh thou art fairer than the evening air
Clad in the beauty of a thousand stars.

The loves of Faustus and Helen are readily allegorized into the passion of the Renaissance for classical beauty, the passion to which all that is not beauty seemed very dross. This is the idea of the second part of "Faust," in which Helen once more became, as she prophesied in the Iliad, a song in the mouths of later men. Almost her latest apparition in English poetry, is in the "Hellenics" of Landor. The sweetness of the character of Helen; the tragedy of the death of Corythus by the hand of his father Paris; and the omnipotence of beauty and charm which triumph over the wrath of Menelaus, are the subjects of Landor's verse. But Helen, as a woman, has hardly found a nobler praise, in three thousand years, than Helen, as a child, has received from Mr. Swinburne in "Atalanta in Calydon." Meleager is the speaker:—

Even such (for sailing hither I saw far hence,
And where Eurotas hollows his moist rock
Nigh Sparta, with a strenuous-hearted stream)
Even such I saw their sisters; one swan-white,
The little Helen, and less fair than she
Fair Clytemnestra, grave as pasturing fawns
Who feed and fear some arrow; but at whiles,
As one smitten with love or wrung with joy,
She laughs and lightens with her eyes, and then
Weeps; whereat Helen, having laughed, weeps too,
And the other chides her, and she being chid speaks naught,
But cheeks and lips and eyelids kisses her
Laughing, so fare they, as in their bloomless bud
And full of unblown life, the blood of gods.

There is all the irony of Fate in Althaeas' reply:

Sweet days befall them and good loves and lords,
Tender and temperate honours of the hearths,
Peace, and a perfect life and blameless bed.